DEFICIT POLITICS

LONGMAN CLASSICS *in* POLITICAL SCIENCE

DEFICIT POLITICS

The Search for Balance in American Politics

SECOND EDITION

DONALD F. KETTL

University of Wisconsin, Madison

With a Foreword by Ross K. Baker, Rutgers University

New York San Francisco Boston
London Toronto Sydney Tokyo Singapore Madrid
Mexico City Munich Paris Cape Town Hong Kong Montreal

Vice President and Publisher: Priscilla McGeehon
Executive Editor: Eric Stano
Senior Marketing Manager: Megan Galvin-Fak
Project Coordination, Text Design, and Electronic Page Makeup: Stet, Inc.
Cover Designer/Manager: Wendy Ann Fredericks
Cover Illustration: © Don Carstens/Brand X Pictures/Picture Quest
Manufacturing Buyer: Lucy Hebard
Printer and Binder: Courier Westford
Cover Printer: Coral Graphics, Inc.

For permissions to use copyrighted material, grateful acknowledgment is
made to the copyright holders within figure legends, which are hereby
made part of this copyright page.

Library of Congress Cataloging-in-Publication Data
Kettl, Donald F.
   Deficit politics : the search for balance in American politics /
Donald F. Kettl; with a foreword by Ross K. Baker.—2nd ed.
      p. cm.
Includes bibliographical references and index.
   ISBN 0-205-29697-1
   1. Budget deficits—United States.   2. Government spending
policy—United States.   3. Taxation—United States.   I. Title.
   HJ2051.K48   2003
   339.5′23′0973—dc21   2002010339

Please visit our website at http://www.ablongman.com

ISBN 0-205-29697-1

1 2 3 4 5 6 7 8 9 10—CRW—05 04 03 02

Contents

v

Foreword

In the popular mind, the words *budget*, *deficit*, and even the more hopeful term *surplus* evoke images of dismal gatherings of dreary men and women hunched over tables in windowless rooms poking at pocket calculators, crunching numbers, splitting hairs, and, conversing in a kind of priestly language unintelligible to ordinary mortals. And, like so much associated with politics in the popular idiom, a slightly sinister aura surrounds them, a hint that no good will come of this murky activity: that ordinary citizens will be fleeced and end up paying more of their treasure in taxes to a wasteful government.

My own initial encounter with budget politics came with a slightly racier aroma left over from the political scandals of the early 1970s that, among other things, caused the resignation of Richard Nixon from the presidency. That encounter was entirely accidental.

In 1975, I had taken my first sabbatical leave from Rutgers University and had joined the staff of Senator Walter F. Mondale, a Democrat from Minnesota who, in 1977, would become Vice President of the United States and in 1984 his party's candidate for president. Mondale assigned me to the staff of a committee that had been created the year before by the Congressional Budget and Impoundment Control Act of 1974. For the first time in history, Congress would have to produce its own budget and not just raise and spend money in a willy-nilly fashion.

The passage of the 1974 Budget Act marked a reversal in a half-century-long trend in which presidents were the dominant force in budget politics. The trend began in 1921 with the passage of the Budget and Accounting Act, which required that each year the president submit a budget to Congress. The act specified that the president's budget had to contain four parts: (1) the amount of money actually spent by the federal government in the previous fiscal year (in those days the fiscal year ran from July 1 to June 30; now it is from October 1 to September 30); (2) the revenues collected in the prior fiscal year; (3) estimates of government spending for the current year, and (4) the president's spending and taxation forecast for the upcoming year. To assist the president in this task, Congress also created the Bureau of the Budget which would be housed in the Treasury Department.

Initially, the Bureau of the Budget maintained a certain operational distance from the White House and gained the reputation of producing more or less reliable estimates. Even after it was moved from Treasury to the new Executive Office of the President in 1939, it was able to maintain a measure of independence. However, beginning with the Johnson Administration and intensifying during the Nixon years (1969–1974) the bureau (renamed the Office of Management and Budget [OMB] in 1970) became increasingly politicized and an extension of the White House itself. Estimates of taxes and spending, which were once regarded as dependable, came to be viewed by Congress as slanted to favor the economic views of the president.

Nixon, moreover, had put himself on a collision course with Congress not only with the Watergate scandal but also with the president's refusal to spend money that had been appropriated by Congress, a practice known as *impoundment.* Congress struck back with the Budget and Impoundment Control Act of 1974, which established a procedure for Congress to come up with devices to thwart impoundment. Of more lasting significance was Congress's decision to formulate its own budget. To this end, it established its own counterpart to the President's Office of Management and Budget, the Congressional Budget Office (CBO), and two new committees that would actually put together Congress's budget, the House Budget Committee and the Senate Budget Committee. It was at this point that I took up my temporary post as a staff member of the Senate's newest standing committee.

Much of the staff of the Senate Budget Committee was housed in a brick building on the corner of First and C Streets, N.E. that had recently been purchased by the Architect of the Capitol. It was just a few steps away from the Rotunda, which was at that time one of the few upscale eating spots on the Senate side of Capital Hill. Before the Budget Committee staff moved into the building, it housed the Carroll Arms Hotel. Located on the first floor of the hotel was an establishment called the Quorum Club, operated by a man named Bobby Baker who had been a staff member to President Lyndon Johnson when he was Majority Leader of the Senate. The Quorum Club was a place where members of Congress would go for romantic liaisons with women who were not their wives. It was in the hotel rooms that once served as the venue for these steamy Capitol trysts that the committee staff responsible for implementing an unprecedented budget process toiled—a setting that would have confirmed in the minds of Americans their most unsavory image of politics, if only they had known the history of the place.

Americans, as a general proposition, have little patience with processes and even less interest in them. Even college and university students who find American politics endlessly fascinating and are drawn to it because of the vividness of the personalities, the grandeur of the American constitutional system, or the uses of power find discussions of procedures not to their liking.

Few academic political scientists, moreover, have devoted themselves to the study of government budgets. It is a topic that has not attracted hordes of practitioners; oddly enough, though, the few who have devoted some part of their careers to the subject are among some of the most respected members of the discipline—scholars such as the late Aaron Wildavsky, Charles E. Lindblom, Richard F. Fenno, Jr., Alan Schick, and the author of *Deficit Politics*, Donald F. Kettl. What these five have in common is the ability to elucidate a process that, in less skilled hands, would remain a body of knowledge known only to specialists.

What lends credibility to Donald F. Kettl's *Deficit Politics* is the author's long-term involvement with practical politics. Regrettably, few academic political scientists venture to "touch the bones." Fearing, perhaps, that they will lose their scholarly detachment and suffer a kind of toxic contamination by their contact with the institutions of government, they cower behind the ramparts of academia and take refuge in abstract theories. While heuristically satisfying, these approaches often seem strangely distant from the way government operates on a day-to-day basis.

Donald Kettl is currently Director of the Robert M. LaFollette Institute of Public Affairs at the University of Wisconsin–Madison. He also serves as a nonresident senior fellow at the respected Brookings Institution in Washington, one of the capital's renowned think tanks.

He received all of his academic training at Yale University. He was elected to Phi Beta Kappa and was awarded his bachelor's degree in 1974. He earned his Ph.D. in 1978—something of a speed record for graduate students. He taught briefly at Columbia University and then moved on to the University of Virginia in 1979. He remained at Virginia for ten years and left in 1989 to become an associate professor at Vanderbilt University and Senior Fellow in the Vanderbilt Institute for Public Policy Studies. In 1990 he received a joint appointment in the Department of Political Science at the University of Wisconsin and at the Robert M. LaFollette School of Public Affairs.

So far, Kettl's curriculum vitae looks like a model of an upwardly mobile academic career. Kettl is a man of many parts, however, and it is his involvement as an adviser, consultant, and leader of study commissions and task forces that makes his career distinctive.

Over a ten-year period Kettl appeared before committees of Congress to testify on a broad array of subjects, ranging from the privatization of government services to the reorganization of the U.S. Department of Energy. By 1996, Kettl was Director of the LaFollette Institute of Public Affairs at the University of Wisconsin–Madison.

His most recent foray into the realm of practical politics was when Wisconsin Governor Tommy Thompson (now Secretary of Health and Human Services in the cabinet of President George W. Bush) named him to head the Commission on State–Local Partnerships for the 21st Century. In September 2000, his commission held a hearing in Madison that was telecast statewide and invited citizens to call in to discuss the problems of state–local relations.

Deficit Politics was published in 1992, on the eve of the election in which President George H.W. Bush would be defeated in his attempt for a second term by Gov. Bill Clinton of Arkansas. Bush's defeat, in part, was attributable to his failure to honor his 1988 pledge at the Houston Convention of the Republican Party. "Read my lips, no new taxes!" Bush proclaimed, paraphrasing Clint Eastwood. By 1990, however, the federal deficit was growing so large that Bush reluctantly agreed to a budget summit with members of Congress in which he was forced to support a tax increase.

Deficit Politics demystified a process that laypersons considered hopelessly arcane and insiders regarded as essentially futile. A belief, which amounted to an article of faith among the elected officials whose job it was to come up with answers for the rapidly mounting deficits of the 1980s and early 1990s, was that somewhere a kind of budgetary "magic bullet" existed that would either put the brake on government spending or infuse politicians with the courage to address realistically the need, from time to time, to raise taxes. The answers, as Donald Kettl was to argue so convincingly, were simple. They just weren't easy.

Kettl begins with the assumption that budget politics are, fundamentally, questions of scope of government, that is, how much government do we want and how much are we willing to pay to get it? Once we make that determination, it would appear simple to raise just enough in taxes to support the level of government services we desire. This simple plan, however, encounters the unpleasant reality that today's public officials are not working with a clean slate. It becomes obvious pretty quickly that about 70 per cent of the federal budget is off-limits because of the existence of entitlement programs such as social security, which has been a benefit program for retirees since 1935 and was augmented in 1964 by Medicare, the health insurance program for the elderly. Add to these sacrosanct programs the need to pay interest on the national debt—an amount that increases every year there is a deficit—and throw in federal retirement programs, and what is left, a category known as "discretionary spending," does not amount to very much.

The magic bullets sought by Congress to curb spending were a series of acts in the 1980s known as Gramm-Rudman-Hollings I, II, and III. These are described in Chapter 5 of *Deficit Politics* as an effort by reformers to "replace the problems of political decision making with a process that will produce the decisions automatically instead." As Kettl points out, the ambitious targets that budget makers set for themselves were never reached. Where hard decisions were called for, gimmicks were preferred, and some of the gimmicks were designed to force Congress to make draconian cuts. Finally, by 1990, the budget experts realized that they were pursuing a will o'the wisp and simply aimed for modest decreases.

Other devices were taken down from the shelf to try to balance the budget. There were such old standbys as the line-item veto, which Congress passed in 1996 and which enabled President Clinton for little more than a year to use to eliminate individual items in appropriations bills that he considered wasteful, and some newer approaches such as a balanced budget amendment to the U.S. Constitution that would have made deficits unconstitutional. The line-item veto was declared unconstitutional in 1998 and the balanced budget amendment never got through the Senate. These failures lead Kettl to conclude, "The promise of a procedural alternative to political struggle is alluring, but in the end it is impossible [because] there is no procedure that cannot be circumvented." Kettl also reminds us that a procedure is not produced by immaculate conception. It is devised by people who stand to gain by its adoption. One example that Kettl cites is Gramm-Rudman-Hollings III, which "produced a massive shift of budgetary power from the Congress to the president simply by giving OMB the prime score keeping role" "Score keeping," as Kettl points out, "determined whether programs were meeting their ceilings or not."

Unquestionably, agreement on what is required to arrive at a balanced budget is complicated by divided government. With Capital Hill and the White House in the hands of opposing parties, the substantial differences in the values of the two parties infuses the budget process with a substantial dose of partisan and ideological fervor. Although efforts have been made to pull the fangs from the process, this effort to departisanize what is essentially an adversary process is, as Donald Kettl points out in Chapter 6, is quite futile. The budget process, as he tells us, is ensnared not only in the ongoing battles between the parties, but also in the enduring tensions in our system of separation of power and checks and balances.

It is political will, above all, that has been in the shortest supply, and that is surely the essential ingredient in budgets—whether they are balanced or in deficit—that properly serve the needs of the

American people. Impatient with the devices used to avoid the application of political will, *Deficit Politics* drives straight to the heart of budget controversies and provides readers with a view uncluttered by sentiment and unclouded by arcane language. It is not merely a classic of budgetary literature but a classic in the larger study of American government.

Suggested Readings

Cole S. Bembeck. *Congress, Human Nature, and the Debt* (New York, N.Y.: Praeger, 1991).

An unusual approach to budget politics in the form of fourteen essays, with a notable foreword by the noted economist James M. Buchanan.

Richard F. Fenno, Jr. *The Power of the Purse* (Boston: Little, Brown, 1966).

The pioneering study of the appropriations process and the source of a typology of the motivations of members of Congress that has become a standard tool of Congressional analysis.

Daniel P. Franklin. *Making Ends Meet* (Washington, D.C.: CQ Press, 1993).

This book can be used to crack the Byzantine code of specialized language and terms of art that have long baffled people who simply want to know how the critical budget process works.

John B. Gilmour. *Reconcilable Differences* (Berkeley, Calif.: University of California Press, 1990).

Gilmour chronicles the Reagan years, which were a critical period in the growth of the federal deficit.

Allen Schick. *The Federal Budget* (Washington, D.C.: The Brookings Institution, 1995).

A widely used guide to the budget process written by one of the leading figures in the field over the past quarter-century.

Study Questions

1. Trace the trends budget process since the inception of the nineteenth century, in terms of the roles of the president and Congress over time.

2. What is your evaluation of the overall effect of the three Gramm-Rudman-Hollings efforts to eliminate the federal deficit?
3. What is the relationship of the federal deficit to the national debt?
4. What was the line-item veto, and what did its advocates claim for it? Do you think that it might have had a major impact on the federal deficit?
5. What is the history of the surplus of the late 1990s, and what has become of it?

Ross K. Baker
Rutgers University

Preface

Until 1998, large and persistent budget deficits ruled the federal government's politics. Elected officials blamed each other for the problem. They seized on the deficit as an example of what was wrong with American politics. They tried to reform the budget process, and they pledged that new policies would avoid future red ink. The constant refrain, however, produced little real change—until the mid-1990s, when a high-stakes duel between Democratic President Bill Clinton and Republican House Speaker Newt Gingrich along with unprecedented economic growth actually wiped out the deficit.

In 1998, the federal government actually showed a surplus. It grew in 1999 and then, for the first time in a generation, the 2000 presidential campaign focused on how best to make use of a budget *surplus* that promised to swell to a trillion dollars over the next decade. President George W. Bush insisted on cutting taxes first and then budgeting what was left and, in a rough battle with congressional Democrats, pushed through most of his plan.

Within months, though, the huge projected surplus disappeared back into a sea of red ink. The economy went into recession. Terrorist attacks on September 11, 2001, brought new federal spending. The trillion dollar surplus largely evaporated and America's short dalliance with surplus politics slipped back into the patterns of deficit politics that had dominated American politics since World War II.

This book charts the history and forces shaping deficit politics. It is anything but a typical book on governmental budgeting. The standard approaches examine what is good or bad about the way budgets are made. They consider how the process works and how it can be improved. They also review the techniques used in making budget decisions. This book is different. I wrote it to explore the questions my students, in more than two decades of courses on budgeting and American politics, were asking—and which standard treatments of the subject often did not answer. I have tried to write the book to answer the questions they asked, in roughly the order they asked them, with the answers that seemed to do the most to satisfy their curiosity—and to stimulate more-sophisticated discussions about what budgeting really is about.

What puzzled my students most was why the political system seemed so profoundly unable to deal with the large and growing deficits of the 1970s and 1980s, how the deficits disappeared in the 1990s, and then why they made a sudden reappearance in the 2000s. Why did the deficit grow, despite the promises of every president to eliminate it? Why did Congress become deadlocked in battle with the president, and why did Congress's own procedures become paralyzed? Why did policy makers simply not buckle down, make the hard decisions, and ease the nation out of the deficit's shadow? Are deficits an inescapable reality of American politics? Having been told over and over by competing partisans that the answers were obvious, and that only political will prevented a solution, students naturally saw continual deficits in a cynical light. At best, government seemed to many students full of weak and spineless officials. At worst, governmental institutions themselves seemed to be straining, even breaking down. Existing budgeting books did not explain very well why these sad results occurred or why the cynical explanations students encountered everywhere were off the mark.

This book probes these puzzles by taking a far broader view of budgeting. Instead of focusing on how budgeting decisions are made, the book seeks to place budgeting within the broad expanse of American politics. The deficit has become the lightning rod of American politics. Virtually every important decision has been drawn to budgeting because every important program has a large financial dimension. The more painful budgetary decisions have become, the more pain has spread across the political landscape. Budgeting thus is a way of understanding the rich fabric of American politics. At the same time, the only way to understand budgeting is to discern how it interconnects with virtually every important issue of American politics.

This book, therefore, has an institutional focus. It also has a strong historical focus, especially through two issues that have emerged to shape budgeting. One is the rise of divided party government, in which, far more often than not, the presidency has been controlled by the Republicans and the Congress by the Democrats. As the Democrats have struggled to regain the presidency and the Republicans have battled to take the Congress, the budget has been squarely in the middle of the conflict. The other issue is the profound but often unnoticed change in the budget itself since the mid-1960s: a shift in who benefits from government programs and from whom the money is raised. Much more money is going, through entitlement programs, to payments to individuals, at the expense of nearly everything else in government. Meanwhile, the tax burden on individuals, especially middle-class citizens, has gradually risen.

Deficit Politics thus focuses most centrally on how the central problems are connected with each other, how causes produce effects, and how the effects then produce new causes. Divided party government affects the budget, and deficit politics plays back into partisan struggles. The changing structure of the budget form budgetary politics, but the patterns of budgetary politics shape the structure of the budget. Most broadly, budgeting and political institutions interconnect. The way institutions work shapes the budget, yet deficit politics changes the way institutions work. Budgeting thus is about far more than decision making. It is the story of American politics—and a very useful way to understand American politics is to poke and probe budgeting.

This approach makes *Deficit Politics* useful for courses both in budgeting and in American politics. For courses in budgeting, it provides an institutional and historical focus not generally available. For courses in public policy, the book explains how budgeting ties in with other policy issues and with the political institutions that make and implement policy. For courses in Congress or the presidency, the book furnishes an important case study on the issue that so often preoccupies the institutions. Finally, for the basic introductory course in American politics, this book tells a lively tale of how the national government makes critical decisions—and how those decisions then shape the national government itself.

In writing this book, I incurred a substantial debt to my students, who continually converged on questions to which they wanted answers and who would not let me off the hook if the answers did not solve their puzzles. I am indebted as well to the many readers of the first edition, who made useful suggestions for improving this new edition. I am deeply grateful as well to my wife, Sue, whose support has been invaluable at every step along the way.

The book offers no magic solutions to the problems of deficit politics. It does, however, debunk the usual miracle cures. The reader may feel, after reading the book, that the answers are even more distant than he or she might have hoped. The book's answer really lies in challenging all of us to fulfill our obligations of citizenship: to think carefully about what kind of government we want, what we want the government to do for us, and what we must do for all of our fellow citizens in return. Its goal is to sharpen the special perspective that budgeting gives, to open up a fascinating window onto American politics.

CHAPTER 1

Politics as Budgeting, Budgeting as Politics

All political issues, sooner or later, become budgetary issues. Government can do almost nothing by fiat. Rather, government usually has to devise clever concoctions—incentives and disincentives, rules and rewards, forms and licenses—to transform bold policy ideas into action. All of these steps require money: to pay government employees to do the job and, more important, to fund the ideas. Politics is thus inevitably about budgeting. Without public money behind government decisions, public policy is an empty concept.

Moreover, all budgetary decisions are inevitably about politics. If there is any basic law of budgeting, it is that everyone wants the benefits of government programs, but no one really wants to pay for them. Indeed, if possible, everyone would like the benefits and have someone else pay the cost. That means budgetary decisions are about scarcity. Policy makers must weigh endless, competing demands for public programs. Students want more money for student loans. Senior citizens want more money for prescription drugs and new treatments. State governments want more federal support for highways, and local governments want more federal and state support for schools. Spending is the happy side of budgeting, but there are always far more ideas for spending money than there could ever be money to pay for them.

At the same time, policy makers constantly scramble to determine how to pay for these programs. Taxes have never been popular. Jesus' disciples were amazed that he chose a tax collector to join his band of apostles. When American colonists wanted to show their displeasure with King George, they tossed tea into Boston harbor rather than pay the taxes on it. Members of Congress for a century

1

have learned they can always grab headlines by attacking the Internal Revenue Service and its tax collectors. Taxing is the unhappy side of budgeting, and citizens have always been reluctant to contribute to the public treasury.

Therefore, conflict is inevitable in public budgeting because budgeting is always about trade-offs. The trade-offs involve puzzles about how to distribute both spending and taxes. They also involve fundamental decisions about how much money the government ought to use for public purposes and how much it ought to leave in the private market. On what programs should governments spend public money? Who receives benefits—and who does not? How should we pay for these programs? Should everyone pay the same, or should some people pay more? These trade-offs require resolving deep-seated conflicts among values. That, in fact, is the very definition of politics. Making those trade-offs is the fundamental job of political institutions and elected officials, especially elected executives (such as presidents, governors, county administrators, and mayors as well as members of Congress, state legislatures, county boards, and city councils).

That is what makes deficit politics such a central element of American government. The level of the deficit—when more money goes out in spending than comes in through taxes—or of the surplus—when more money comes in than goes out—is the single most-watched gauge of budgeting's big trade-offs. It also is the most-followed measure of government's connection with the economy. To peel apart the layers of government budgeting, therefore, is to gain a keen insight into the most important issues of American politics: how elected officials and their institutions work through value conflicts and, ultimately, how American governments affect all of us.

A *deficit* occurs when the government's spending exceeds its income. A *surplus* occurs when income exceeds expenditures. Except for 1969, the federal budget was in deficit from 1961 until 1998—and, in fact, for most years since World War II.

In the late 1990s, after decades of political rhetoric and hard decisions, the federal government managed to eliminate the deficit. The victory proved short-lived, however. The combination of the 2001 terrorist attacks and a weakened economy pushed the budget back into the red. Nagging questions produce no good answers. Even after accounting for the shocks of 2001, why can't we, once and for all, solve the deficit problem? Why can't the president produce a budget that is not declared "dead on arrival" immediately on its release? Why can't Congress meet its deadlines, approve a budget, and avoid late-night sessions and shoot-outs with the president? Why can't the parties behave responsibly, by negotiating a way out instead of using budgetary disputes for petty, short-term advantage? Why can't we make the hard choices required to balance the budget? Most simply, why can't we get our system of government to work, in this most central of all governmental activities?

All too often, the budget-making process seems to represent government at its worst instead of its best. The battles between the president and the Congress, the squabbling between Democrats and Republicans, the campaign promises of budget balance that evaporate into higher taxes and spending—all are powerful symbols of a government struggling to resolve what often seem irresolvable problems. Worst of all, despite firm pledges and brave predictions, the budget deficit doesn't seem to go away, and the national debt spirals ever upward. Why can't we do a better job of governing ourselves?

This book pokes and probes these questions. It builds on two simple ideas. First, the budget is such a contentious issue because it is the one place in American government where almost everything of importance comes together. Nearly anything we want government to do requires money, and getting the money brings everyone sooner or later to the budgetary conflict. Budgetary decisions are so hard because the issues are so big.

Second, in understanding how budgeting envelops so many important issues, we gain a very useful perspective on the workings of American politics. Engineers test the systems they design in wind tunnels and other torture chambers that subject their ideas to great stress. Budgeting is the wind tunnel of American politics. In one place it brings together the important issues and biggest stresses that challenge the functioning of government. The study of the budget reveals both the best and the worst of the important institutions, processes, and policies of our national government. The budget is thus more than a story of decision making. It is a unique window into the very core of American democracy. The view through this window is not always pretty, but the struggles strike to the enduring challenge of balancing economics—making the best use of the public's money—with politics to find consensus on policy strategies.

The 1990 Budget Summit

In late 1990, as Congress was struggling over the 1991 federal budget, U.S. Senator David Pryor (D-Ark.) was flying back to Washington. The passenger next to him was curious about whether he worked for the federal government. "As a matter of fact," Senator Pryor replied, "I do. I'm a United States Senator." The passenger replied, "Well, if you don't mind, I don't want to sit with you" and changed seats to avoid rubbing elbows.[1]

Rarely had a political battle so enraged the American public. Late-night sessions, full of name-calling and partisan baiting, occupied Congress. Proposals for new taxes rose and fell, while nearby halls outside congressional hearings were clogged with lobbyists. Many citizens feared that the special interests would hijack the process to benefit their particular constituencies, while the elderly worried that the costs of their medical care would rise. The October 1 deadline for passing the new budget came and went with the work unfinished. President Bush haggled with Democratic congressional leaders over temporary extensions of the government's spending authority, and, when the talks disintegrated, the entire government was shut down. It was not, to put it mildly, a happy time for the American political system.

Had this been but an isolated episode, the battle would have been bad enough. The 1990 quarrel, however, was just one more in a series of budgetary crises that had characterized budgeting during the 1980s. Only once in the 1980s did Congress get its budgetary work done before the deadline, and every budget debate was filled with deep, sometimes ugly rancor. It was bad enough that President Bush and the Congress had such a difficult time in 1990 finding agreement on the budget. Even worse, it was one more chapter in continuing budget battles—and the hint of more battles to come.

Worst of all, analysts and citizens alike worried that the struggles over the budget marked a breakdown of the lawmaking process and, perhaps, of American political institutions. Why are budget decisions so difficult? Why can't elected officials make the hard choices they are elected to make? Are these problems the consequence of a deep crisis in the American political system?

At the beginning of the 1988 presidential campaign, Republican candidate George Bush knew that he had to separate himself from the Democratic challenger, Michael Dukakis. As vice president under Ronald Reagan for eight years, he had the obvious advantage of the president's popularity. America was at peace and enjoying the longest peacetime economic expansion (to that point) in American history. The Democrats, meanwhile, continued to suffer their continuing problems in presidential election campaigns. In the 1984 election, Walter Mondale looked at endless budget deficits and said, bluntly, that balancing the budget would require tax increases. President Reagan charged that Mondale was yet one more of the "tax and tax, spend and spend" Democrats, and he easily defeated Mondale in the election. Dukakis inherited the ghost of Democratic candidates past, the free-spending and high-taxing label that the Republicans had so skillfully stitched onto their campaigns. To cap off the campaign, candidate George Bush made a blunt promise borrowed in part from the movies. "Read my lips!" he challenged. "No new taxes." Dukakis refused to take the same pledge. That tax issue helped lead George Bush to the White House in January 1989.

By mid-1990, however, the economy began weakening rapidly. The budget deficit, projected in the president's budget to be only about $64 billion, began spiraling upward. Everyone agreed that a new budget was needed, but neither the president nor the Congress wanted to take the first step. President Bush had his "no new taxes" pledge, while the Democrats in Congress had the "tax-and-tax, spend-and-spend" noose around their necks. Both sides agreed that the only way to resolve the problem was to meet in a budget summit and tie both sides politically to the results. When the summit began in early May, President Bush announced that there would be "no preconditions." The Democrats understood this as a subtle message that the president would consider a tax increase as well as spending reductions.[2] That signal was critical. The weakening economy was

pushing the deficit up quickly, and simple arithmetic suggested to the negotiators that bringing the deficit down significantly would require both tax increases and spending cuts. Their initial targets, in fact, were a $40 billion reduction in the deficit during the first year, and a $500 billion deficit cut over the next five years.

After having been thrashed in two presidential elections on the tax issue, they welcomed Bush's announcement as a significant retreat. Within days of the announcement, however, White House Chief of Staff John Sununu suggested to reporters that the president's "no preconditions" statement really meant that the Democrats could pass new taxes—but that the White House stood ready to veto them. The Bush administration signaled that it would not accept political responsibility for any tax increase. The administration might thus be able to keep its no-new-taxes pledge, win a deficit reduction, and blame the Democrats for any new taxes. The Democratic congressional leaders, of course, quickly smelled the trap and began plotting to outmaneuver the White House. They worked out a counterstrategy: they would drag their heels in the summit and push the debate to the very last moment. They hoped that would gain the greatest leverage over the president. If things fell apart, they believed they could portray White House negotiators as the villains who wrecked the summit.

These tactics produced an intricate minuet. In public, both sides struggled to position themselves as champions of the people, working hard to reduce the deficit while protecting taxpayers from the government's heavy hand. Behind the scenes, each side maneuvered to back the other into one of two corners: either taking responsibility for a tax increase or accepting blame for the higher deficit if the talks collapsed.

The summit negotiators disappeared behind closed doors and planned to emerge at the last moment with a deficit-reduction plan. If they succeeded, both sides would be able to claim credit, and, because everyone's fingerprints would be on the deal, neither side could blame the other for its contents. To make it work, though, the Democrats insisted on a promise from President Bush that he would not walk away from the deal and leave the Democrats holding a tax-increase bag. At the end of June, the signal came back from the president. On the bulletin board of the White House press room

appeared a short statement recognizing the need for "tax revenue increases." Washington reporters were quick to point out the paradox that this retreat from the "no new taxes" campaign pledge occurred through a seemingly innocuous note, containing words that no one at the White House dared even say out loud. This flight from the president's no-new-taxes pledge energized the budget summit.

Soon, though, the summit confronted two important issues. On one front, conservative House Republicans, many of whom had also taken the no-new-taxes promise and remained unwilling to back away from it, promised to fight any deficit agreement that included tax hikes. On another front, Iraq invaded Kuwait. The strong stand President Bush took against Saddam Hussein drove his popularity to near-record levels. White House negotiators believed that both issues gave them powerful cards to play. The House Republicans' opposition to new taxes could force the Democrats to accept larger cuts in their favorite social programs, and the president's mounting popularity could make the deal stick. White House Chief of Staff Sununu, in fact, confidently took one Democratic plan, crumpled it into a ball, and tossed it over his shoulder.[3] President Bush and his negotiators believed that, in this card game, they were holding the aces.

The summiteers adjourned to Andrews Air Force Base, just outside Washington. After haggling over the shape of the table and the color of the security badges, the summit finally got to work, but every idea proved a dead-end canyon. Some House Republican leaders opposed any plan that included tax increases. Other Republican negotiators argued that any summit deal ought to include President Bush's 1988 campaign pledge to reduce the federal tax on capital gains. A lower capital-gains tax rate, President Bush had argued in the campaign, would increase incentives to invest in the economy and thus fuel economic growth. Computer estimates, however, showed that this change would reduce government revenues after several years and actually increase the deficit. Democratic leaders countered that they would give President Bush his capital-gains tax cut only if he matched it with new tax increases on the wealthy, but the White House rejected that deal. Meanwhile, Democratic leaders were willing to accept Republican demands that they cut their favorite programs, but certainly not if it became a ruse to leave them with the blame. With so many suspicions, the summit collapsed.

A *capital gain* is income produced through the increase in the value of capital investments, such as stocks, bonds, or real estate. If an investor buys a stock for $100, for example, and sells it five years later for $150, the $50 increase in value is a capital gain. The 1986 tax reform act had fixed the capital-gains tax at the same rates as for other kinds of income.

Both the White House and congressional leaders wanted to forge some kind of agreement. A smaller group of key Republican and Democratic congressional leaders, this time without some of the more contentious members of Congress, began a new series of meetings with Chief of Staff Sununu and Budget Director Richard Darman. The October 1 deadline for the beginning of the new budget year, called the fiscal year, was quickly approaching, and both sides were becoming more desperate for a deal. The Democrats offered to give President Bush his capital-gains tax cut, this time if he agreed to increase the income tax rate for the wealthiest Americans from 28 to 32 percent. The White House refused.

The *fiscal year* is the government's budget year. The 1974 budget reform act changed the fiscal year beginning date from July 1 to October 1, in the hope that the White House and Congress could more easily come to agreement on each year's budget. It certainly has not worked out that way.
The federal fiscal year thus begins on October 1 and ends the following September 30. The fiscal year is numbered with the year in which it ends. Thus, fiscal year 2004 begins on October 1, 2003, and ends on September 30, 2004.

At the very last moment, on September 30, the negotiators emerged with a different plan. The summit agreement raised new revenue through large increases in the gasoline and alcohol taxes. The White House negotiators accepted this part of the plan because they interpreted the president's no-new-taxes promise to mean no increase in income tax rates, which the summit agreement would not affect. The Democrats took pleasure in arguing that a tax was a tax, no matter what it was called. Both sides thus claimed victory on the revenue side. On the spending side, the summit agreement called for big cuts in the Medicare program, produced in part by lower fees paid to doctors and hospitals, in part by much higher fees paid by Medicare recipients, and in part through the expansion of the taxes that finance the program.

In the *Medicare* program, the federal government finances medical care for the nation's senior citizens. Individuals over the age of 65 are eligible for government-paid doctor visits and hospital care. The program is financed through the payroll tax, listed on most paycheck stubs as FICA (Federal Insurance Contribution Act). Since 1990, employers and employees have each paid 7.65 percent of their earned income to finance social security and Medicare, 1.45 percent for Medicare and 6.20 percent for social security. Self-employed individuals pay both shares—15.3 percent. Workers do not pay social security tax on wages above $84,900 (in 2002), but they do pay the health insurance tax. Everyone has to pay these taxes from the first dollar of earned income, even if no federal or state income tax is owed. Other income, such as interest from savings accounts or from capital gains, is not subject to the tax.

The White House and the congressional leaders breathed an enormous sigh of relief, confident that their work was finally done. To keep government going until work could be completed, they fashioned a continuing resolution. (When passed by Congress and signed by the president, a *continuing resolution* maintains government programs at agreed-on levels until the regular budget is passed.) The negotiators, though, greatly underestimated the reaction to the plan. Many conservative House Republicans charged that the White House had sold out on the tax issue and pledged to vote against the budget. Many liberal Democrats attacked the plan as unfair to the poor and the middle class, through the new taxes on gasoline and alcohol, and as especially unfair to the elderly, because of the new Medicare fees. To build support for the plan, President Bush appeared on television and asked Americans to urge their members of Congress to vote for the agreement. A flood of calls, telegrams, and letters arrived on Capitol Hill, but in overwhelming numbers they urged that the agreement be killed.

Early in the morning of Friday, October 5, the members of the House agreed with the thousands of their constituents who had opposed the summit agreement. The death of the summit plan, however, threatened to shut the government down. The continuing resolution had expired on Friday evening at midnight. Federal law forbids the government to spend money without congressional authorization, and without a budget or a new continuing resolution the government would be out of money. President Bush refused to sign a new resolution without a budget, and neither side could produce one. Virtually all functions of the government thus were forced to close. When visitors arrived the next morning at Washington's National Zoo to see the pandas, they discovered the zoo closed and the pandas locked in their house. Museums all over the capital were bolted shut, and television cameras hovered around irate tourists. What had begun as the politics of principle had degenerated into profound embarrassment and bad theater. Over the weekend, embarrassed congressional leaders and White House officials agreed on a new continuing resolution. By Monday morning, the federal government was back at work and congressional leaders began to plot new strategies for the budget.

This time, though, the Democrats sensed that they had the Republicans on the run. First, President Bush had promised no new taxes, but he had finally agreed to accept "tax revenue increases." Then President Bush insisted on a capital-gains tax cut as part of any budget deal, but then backed away. He said he would not sign a continuing resolution without progress on a deficit agreement, but then relented in time to put the government back to work. President Bush's refusal to sign a new continuing resolution, intended to show his resolve, had only fueled popular resentment. The Democrats believed that they had won the upper hand.

In the process, they discovered the "fairness" issue, which involved taxing the rich to reduce taxes and increase benefits for the poor and the middle class. House Democrats concocted a devilish new plan. As the price for the president's capital gains tax *cut*, which would principally benefit the wealthy, they would *increase* other taxes on the well-to-do. They would impose new luxury taxes on expensive planes, boats, cars, and furs; a higher income tax rate for upper-income persons; and a special new tax on millionaires. Their argument was that if the rich received new tax breaks, it would only be fair if they helped finance the deficit-reduction plan. The Democrats framed a choice as millionaires versus Medicare recipients and left no doubt about which side they were on.

This plan presented President Bush and his advisers with an unpleasant choice. They could swallow the Democrats' plan and completely capitulate on the tax issue. That was politically unacceptable. Having worked so hard through three presidential elections to establish the tax issue, the Republicans were not about to bargain it away to support the Democrats' plan. If they opposed the Democrats' scheme, however, they would have to come up with an equivalent amount of money somewhere else and risk being portrayed as protectors of the very rich, enemies of the elderly and the middle class, and opponents of fairness. To reject both options would mean abandoning any hope of real deficit reduction, and the worsening deficit picture made that unthinkable. In late January, administration officials had projected that the deficit for fiscal year 1991 would be $64 billion. By late September, the estimate had risen to $294 billion, and the nation's financiers were getting very nervous. Administration officials strongly believed that *something* had to be done about the deficit and that to save face this "something" had to be a $500 billion package over the next five years. The snare that Chief of Staff Sununu had set earlier in the year now threatened to trap him instead.

Some of President Bush's advisers, including Vice President Dan Quayle, urged him simply to walk away from the talks. A bad deal, they warned, was worse than no deal. After the November 1990 congressional elections, they reasoned, the president could start anew. Other advisers, led by Budget Director Darman, warned that the nation's economic future depended on making immediate and significant progress against the deficit. The internal White House turmoil and the squabbles among Republicans in the House convinced Democratic leaders they had won. They retreated from their insistence on the special tax for millionaires and agreed to reduce the capital-gain tax slightly. In return, they demanded an increase in the top income tax rate to 31 percent from 28 percent. They insisted on lower deductions for those making more than $100,000. They increased taxes on gasoline and alcohol, and they increased charges Medicare beneficiaries had to pay; in both cases, though, the new taxes were not nearly as large as in the original summit plan. White House officials reluctantly conceded that this was the best they were likely to do and decided to go along.

The Democrats declared victory. They had backed President Bush away from his no-new-taxes promise and also from his fallback position, that "no new taxes" really meant no increase in tax *rates*. They had given the president in return only a modest reduction in the capital-gain tax rate. Both sides, meanwhile, contented themselves by arguing that the plan would reduce the deficit by $40 billion in fiscal year 1991 and by almost, but not quite, $500 billion by fiscal year 1996.

The Democrats were satisfied with the results of the shoot-out, but most voters viewed the battle as an embarrassment for both sides. The spectacle of late-night congressional debates, closed museums, vaporized read-my-lips promises, long lines of special interests in Capitol corridors, partisan squabbling, and White House disarray all fueled a virulent antigovernment mood among many citizens. The telephone lines at talk radio stations lit up with bitter complaints about politicians. Citizens wished a pox on both the Congress and the White House. Even President Bush's personal popularity, raised by his strong stand against Saddam Hussein, plummeted sixteen points in just two weeks after Congress's late-night rejection of the plan.

President Bush, of course, was not about to surrender the high ground to the Democrats. Soon after the battle ended, he pledged "remedial work" to reclaim leadership of his party. He admitted to "serious regrets" about "being forced" to abandon the no-new-taxes pledge, and promised that he would "absolutely" not budge on further tax increases. Any new tax increases would have to be passed by the Democrats "over my dead veto," he promised, "because it ain't going to happen, I'll guarantee you." He concluded, "I'm girding up my loins to go into battle to beat back the tax attempts that I think are coming. Because I think the American people are fed up with it."[4] From the smoke of 1990's budget brawl thus came the first shots for the budget battles that were to follow, in 1991 and thereafter.

When President Bush's next budget appeared in February 1991, his plan for a big cut in the capital-gain tax was back, and the old issues began smoldering yet again.

What happened during late 1990 was the result of more than just late-night political shenanigans. Many observers, both ordinary citizens and sophisticated pundits, saw in the bruising battle a symptom of a far deeper problem. Weekly news magazines bluntly asked whether government worked anymore. *U.S. News and World Report*, for example, ran a cover story, "Throw the Bums Out!" The magazine noted, "Government is paralyzed, and voters are angry." Inside, the magazine's story contended, "If this were a European parliament, the government would already have resigned in disgrace." In the budget battle, "both sides are scrambling in a manic pursuit worthy of the Keystone Kops," characters from the old silent black-and-white movie days known for chasing wildly around while accomplishing nothing.[5]

The 1990 budget episode marked the third time in a decade that the government had been shut down. It was another occasion for bitter partisan wrangling. It was yet another chapter in the lost promise to balance the federal budget, a budget that was last balanced in fiscal year 1969 and balanced only eight times since the end of World War II. The budget battles seemed eternal, but real progress was elusive. Worse yet, the political system seemed incapable of dealing with the problem. It was little wonder, then, that questions arose about whether deficit politics signaled much deeper problems of governance.

The 2001 Response to Terrorism

George Bush's son struggled with a similar budget battle a decade later. In the aftermath of the September 11, 2001, terrorist attacks on New York and Washington, George W. Bush proposed a three-part recovery plan. Bush initially proposed a $20 billion emergency fund. Swept up in concern for their constituents and a determination to act quickly, Congress trumped the president and doubled the amount to $40 million—$20 million for emergency response and a buildup of intelligence and military forces and another $20 million in short-term aid for New York, western Pennsylvania (where one of the planes seized by the terrorists crashed), and the Washington area.

Within two weeks of the attacks, Congress also quickly passed a $15 billion plan to assist the nation's airlines, whose business was crippled by the terrorist attacks. One third of the money went in direct grants to the airlines to help alleviate their financial hemorrhage. The other $10 billion was earmarked for loan guarantees. A board, comprising Federal Reserve Board Chairman Alan Greenspan, Treasury Secretary Paul H. O'Neill, Transportation Secretary Norman Y. Mineta, and U.S. Comptroller General David M. Walker, had the power to write the rules for deciding who would be allowed to borrow how much. The money was not a gift. The airlines would be allowed to borrow money. If an airline could not repay the loan, the federal government would guarantee the lenders that they would get their money back. In exchange for the guarantee, the federal government would negotiate a partial ownership of the airline.

Airline lobbyists had descended on the Capitol the day after the attacks. The airlines were already having a very bad year, and industry executives feared that the attacks would drive away fliers and push several big airlines into bankruptcy. They responded with a concerted lobbying campaign, "the most high-level surgical strike I have ever seen," one lobbyist said. Indeed, "It was masterful," said Sen. Peter G. Fitzgerald (R-Ill.), who cast the Senate's lone vote against the rescue package. "The airline industry made a full-court press to convince Congress that giving them billions in taxpayer cash was the only way to save the republic."[6] The airline lobbyists, in fact, had been having a busy and successful year. They fought off a proposal for a passengers' bill of rights, and they convinced President Bush to employ rarely used powers to block a strike by airline employees. The airlines had been hit hard, both financially and emotionally, by the terrorist attacks—but, for that matter, so too had the tourist, restaurant, and hotel industries. Yet the airlines were uniquely successful in winning immediate federal support to stem their financial losses.

The third element of Bush's plan, however, immediately ran into serious problems. He joined with congressional Republicans to propose an economic stimulus program to jump-start the economy. The economy had enjoyed the longest peacetime expansion in American history—longer, in fact, than the one during the Reagan-Bush years. With the terrorist attacks, however, came disturbing signs that the economy was weakening. Signs were emerging that a recession might be under way. Unemployment was rising and the Federal Reserve, worried about the slowdown, had cut interest rates repeatedly to spur economic growth. Bush worried that the attacks would push the economy from weakness into a deep recession. Journalists and advisers alike reminded him that an economic slowdown had proven political poison for his father, and Bush determined to move aggressively. "The president is deeply concerned about the economy and the people who have lost their jobs," White House spokeswoman Claire Buchan told reporters. "He believes he needs to work with Republicans and Democrats to develop solutions to address the problem."[7]

Economists define a *recession* as two consecutive quarters—six months—of economic contraction. They reserve the term *depression* to refer to severe economic downturns characterized by low sales by merchants, high rates of business failures, and high levels of unemployment. Recessions occur with regularity. The last American depression was in the 1930s.

Three weeks after the terrorist attacks, Bush launched a $75 billion "economic security" plan, to fit with his airline security and homeland security initiatives. He argued that almost all of the plan—$60 billion—ought to go to tax cuts instead of increased federal spending. Some low-income taxpayers had not received the same $300 tax rebates sent to other taxpayers earlier in the year, or they had received no rebate at all. Bush proposed that these taxpayers get an immediate rebate. He also proposed a speedup of income tax cuts passed earlier in 2001 but not scheduled to take effect until 2004, and he recommended a package of business tax cuts that would increase incentives for industry to invest in new equipment.

Democrats promptly criticized the Bush plan. They had fought Bush's tax cuts earlier in 2001 because, they contended, they benefited the rich. By using most of stimulus money for speeding up future tax cuts and providing more tax breaks to business, all of the battles they had fought and lost months before resurfaced. But two things had changed since the springtime budget battles. The terrorist attacks focused attention on the weakening economy, and everyone was eager to act. In addition, though, the political dynamics had profoundly changed. After a series of spats with the White House, Republican Senator Jim Jeffords from Vermont decided during the summer of 2001 to become an independent. That tipped the Senate from a 50–50 split, in which Vice President Cheney cast the deciding vote, to fifty Democrats, forty-nine Republicans, and one independent. When Jeffords decided to join with the Democrats in organizing the Senate, the Republicans lost control and their ability to push through the president's economic security plan was greatly weakened.

Tax breaks to help companies buy new computers would spur production and help the economy, Republicans argued. Democrats urged passage of assistance for the unemployed, including health insurance. The Republicans countered with a plan to give tax credits to people who could not find jobs; the Democrats tried to trump them by pressing for an expansion of the Medicaid program to cover workers who did not receive health insurance from their employers. Meanwhile, special interests flooded the debate with their own plans. They quickly took a cue from the airline industry and portrayed every idea for new spending increases or tax cuts as an "economic security" initiative. Everyone had ideas about how to spend money. The terrorist attacks put many old ideas as well as some new ones on the table and provided a political case for pursuing them. Democrats saw this, combined with their takeover of the Senate, as an opportunity to push back the Republicans. Republicans, alarmed at the prospect of having their agenda scuttled, fought back.

The president's budget officials, along with outside economists, were worried about the impact of these plans on the budget. Just a month before the terrorist attacks, budget officials had projected a surplus of $176 billion for fiscal year 2002. Even without the cost of the stimulus package, the projected surplus had dwindled to just $1 billion and the weakening economy threatened to push the budget into deficit. A stimulus package would swell the deficit to perhaps $100 billion or more. The ten-year forecast, which as recently as

January 2002 had estimated a total budget surplus of $5.6 trillion, now showed a surplus below $2 trillion. Congress and the Clinton administration had made hard budget decisions during the 1990s, and the budget had finally begun to show a surplus. The terrorist attacks and the economic slowdown, however, undid years of work in just months. Democrats, who had argued in the spring that Bush's tax cuts would bring back deficits, gleefully blamed Republicans. Some Republicans, who had hoped they could restore budgetary balance, worried that inescapable political pressure would destroy fiscal discipline. The economic security debate quickly deteriorated into a political battle just like the one a decade earlier—one in which congressional Republicans and Democrats had battled for tactical advantage.

Unlike the 1990 struggle, however, the Republicans and Democrats fought to a draw. Democrats tried to paint Republicans as foes of working people and protectors of the rich. Republicans argued that Senate Democratic Leader Tom Daschle (D-S.D.) was an obstructionist. Bush Deputy Press Secretary Scott McClellan told reporters, "We're . . . fighting a recession here at home, and that's right at the top of the agenda."[8] Daschle countered by attacking Bush's tax plan, saying, "The tax cut failed to prevent a recession; it probably made the recession worse."[9] The new year started the same way the old one ended, with both sides positioning themselves for the battle over control of Congress that would be decided in the 2002 midterm congressional elections.

Critics on both sides had quietly breathed a sigh of relief at the standoff. The tax rebate for lower-income workers, for example, would not have taken effect until the spring of 2002. The impact of new tax breaks would likely have taken much longer. By that point, economists estimated, the economy would be in the midst of recovery. That, economists worried might be exactly the wrong medicine because it might fuel inflation. The delay, they concluded, was actually a good thing because it prevented pumping too much money into the economy just as it was beginning to take off. Democrats were glad that they had stopped more Republican tax cuts, and they relished blaming Republicans for pushing the federal budget back into deficit. Republicans were glad they had restrained new Democratic spending programs, especially for health care, and they enjoyed portraying Daschle—rumored to be a possible presidential candidate—as a roadblock to the country's response to terrorism. Thus, in economic terms, it was a case that no news was good news. In political terms, it was a case that no news gave both parties a chance to portray the other in an unflattering light. In both cases, it was the essence of deficit politics.

Inflation is an increase in the price for goods and services. As inflation increases, a worker's wage buys less. The cost of everything from cars and gasoline to health care and food increases. Workers often demand higher wages to keep up, and that can lead to a spiral—higher wages can push up prices, and higher prices can push up wages. The same forces can drive up the cost of the government's goods and services and strain government's ability to finance its operations.

Does Government Work?

These cases breed tough questions. Why can't elected officials simply buckle down and work through budget issues? Do they lack courage? Is the process captive of special interests? Are elected officials more focused on partisan advantage than on good policy? Can the process be fixed in a way to force decisions that decision makers do not want to make? Most of all, can a government that cannot keep its financial process in order deal with other issues well? Indeed, are these cases a sign that government simply does not work well? The story of budgeting in the American political system is not a pretty one and, especially since the late 1970s, it has gotten uglier.

We naturally resist the idea that budgeting has to be so messy and seek some way to make the process smoother, the results more attractive. As we explore the problems, we will turn first to why the budget matters and why its problems prove so difficult to solve. We move next to different approaches for making budgeting more rational. Reforms of the budgetary process have been a continual concern of government officials. From these issues of reform, we shift to the fundamental problems of governmental institutions and governance of the nation.

Along the way, we will be using deficit politics to explore two deep and important issues. Federal budgeting is important in its own right, because it shapes the way the government relates to the rest of American—and indeed the world—society. Budgeting is fundamentally a decision about how much of society's resources we want to take from the private sector to use for problems of broader public interest. These decisions are central to the purpose of government, so it is scarcely surprising that they arouse such intense political struggles. These struggles, in turn, tell us much about the processes and institutions that govern us. Budgeting is a prism that breaks apart, for careful study, the critical issues of American politics. The first issue the prism identifies for us is why the deficit is such an important—and difficult—policy problem.

Notes

1. Mark Barnhill, "Voters Angry," *Wisconsin State Journal*, November 4, 1990, p. 1F.
2. For an excellent review of the issue, from which part of this discussion is drawn, see Alan Murray and Jackie Calmes, "How the Democrats, with Rare Cunning, Won the Budget War," *Wall Street Journal*, November 5, 1990, p. A1.
3. Ibid., p. A6.
4. Andrew Rosenthal, "Reacting to Vote, President Renews Anti-Tax Pledge," *New York Times*, November 9, 1990, p. A1.
5. *U.S. News and World Report*, October 22, 1990, vol. 109, cover and p. 28.
6. Quoted in Leslie Wane and Michael Moss, "Bailout for Airlines Showed the Weight of a Mighty Lobby," *New York Times*, October 10, 2001, p. A1.
7. Glenn Kessler, "Bush to Work with Congress on Economic Stimulus Plan; Administration Says Boost Is Needed to Offset Fallout," *Washington Post*, September 27, 2001, p. A3.
8. Edwin Chen, "Bush to Stump for Economic Recovery Plan," *Los Angeles Times*, January 4, 2002, p. A24.
9. Glenn Kessler, "Daschle: Bush's Tax Cut to Blame for Vanishing Surplus," WashingtonPost.com, January 4, 2002.

CHAPTER 2

Why Deficits Matter

The federal deficit has become the most prominent symbol in American politics. It is the backdrop against which every policy idea plays. Will a new program increase spending and risk swelling the deficit? Could a tax cut fuel the economy and produce a surplus? The budget is the touchstone of every policy issue and debate. It is the foundation question of whether we can afford new programs, and it is the measure of every program's effect. Indeed, there is perhaps no better symbol of what government does and how it does it than the budget and its deficit.

The shadow of the budget has not always been this long. Before the Great Depression of the 1930s, the fundamental norm of federal budgeting was balance.[1] Although neither the president nor the Congress successfully balanced the federal budget every year, there was the clear expectation that the budget *should* be balanced and that a deficit ought to be the rare exception to this policy. In fact, until the Great Depression, Congress and the president followed this norm most of the time. During wars, which always quickly increased spending, deficits were large. For long periods in between, however, the federal government ran surpluses—sometimes huge ones. The proper thing to do, nearly everyone agreed, was to balance the budget. When economic conditions permitted, furthermore, the conventional wisdom argued that the government should run an even bigger surplus to pay off previous borrowing. Along the way, these conventional notions disappeared as economic theory matured. New economic ideas changed the way that policy makers thought about deficits and, somewhat accidentally, set the stage for the large deficits of the past decades.

Just what is the budget "deficit," and how does it relate to
the "national debt"? Simply put, the budget *deficit* is the amount
by which, in any given year, the government's expenditures
(often called *outlays*) exceed receipts. A surplus occurs when
receipts exceed outlays. When the government runs a deficit,
it must borrow the money from investors, both at home and
abroad. The amount borrowed is called the *national debt*. New
deficits increase the debt, and surpluses are used to reduce the
debt. The national debt thus represents the government's
accumulated borrowing over time. The deficit, on the other
hand, is a snapshot of the government's outlays and receipts in
a single year.

Classical economics and traditional notions about good financial
management have long argued for balancing the budget and, whenever possible, paying off the debt. In the early days, officials argued
that a large debt would make investors, especially abroad, less likely
to help finance the new nation's expenses. The larger the debt, the
less likely that investors would ever be paid off. In fact, one of the
first decisions the founding fathers had to make was whether the new
national government would be responsible for the debts incurred
by the states in fighting the war for independence. Alexander
Hamilton, the first secretary of the treasury, began his term by
arguing that the nation had no choice. To repudiate the debt would
mean that no one would lend new money, and if the nation could
not borrow it would never be able to grow.

These beginning concepts set the stage for 150 years of federal
financial management. If a balanced budget was impossible—because
of a war, for example—elected officials saw the situation as regret-
table and resolved to produce a budget surplus as soon as possible to
begin reducing the debt. The basic idea remained the same: A nation
that made good on its promises would always be able to borrow. The
national debt always grew more quickly than it was paid off. In large
part, this was because wars, such as the War of 1812 and the Civil
War, greatly increased the nation's borrowing, far more than the
nation could pay back in short order. The underlying norm of budget
balance never waned, however. If the debt could not be paid off
immediately, government officials nevertheless maintained the idea

that the deficit ought to be reduced, and whenever possible they tried to do so.

So strong was this norm of balance, in fact, that when the economy crumbled during the Great Depression and budget deficits increased, President Herbert Hoover proposed a tax increase to bring the budget back into balance. Classical economics did not suggest that governmental activity affected employment in the private sector. Hoover believed there was little that the government could or should do about the problem except keep its own financial house in order. Prudent management of federal finances, he contended, would give the economy the chance to recover. Economists later argued that this was precisely the wrong remedy and the wrong time. To Hoover and his advisers, whose views were shaped by the norm of budgetary balance, there seemed no other alternative.[2]

Government Management of the Economy

By the time President Franklin D. Roosevelt took office in March 1933, the American economy was in shambles. Banks were closing and some families lost all of their savings. Unemployment spiraled upward until nearly one of every four people in the workforce was without a job. With the problems so huge, Roosevelt and his advisers believed that government had no choice but to put conventional theories aside. The government, they argued, had to take some action to get the country moving again. Reassuring words from the president in fireside chats would not be enough. Instead, as one economic adviser put it, "the only way we could get out of the depression was through government action in placing purchasing power in the hands of people who were in need of it."[3]

This was a truly radical idea. To this point, the government's budget had been narrowly thought of as a mechanism for raising enough money to pay for the government's programs, and that was as far as things went. Conventional economic wisdom held that the governmental policy did not play much of a role in the economy. Furthermore, according to classical economics, downturns such as the Great Depression were self-correcting. The economy regularly went through cycles. If the economy expanded too quickly, the balloon would eventually pop, as it did in the late 1920s. If it began slowing, wages would drop low enough to encourage manufacturers to resume production. In the long run, the economy on its own would reach an equilibrium, at which everyone who wanted to work would be able to. At this equilibrium, the economy would be at full employment.

Roosevelt and his advisers concluded that they simply could not wait for the long run. People were hungry and out of work. They concluded that the government could—and should—use its ability to borrow money to launch new employment programs. Even if the programs were make-work, individuals could at least do something productive and earn a wage to feed their families. The strategy of Roosevelt's New Deal, of course, meant that the government would inevitably have to run a deficit. The Roosevelt administration did not suggest that the government should run perpetual deficits. In fact, the president and his staff saw the deficits as a short-term necessity to cure the Depression, and they fully intended to return to the classical approach when the Depression was over. From this rough-and-ready logic came Roosevelt's New Deal, a collection of federal programs devoted to building new roads, constructing new buildings, and putting Americans back to work.

Keynes and Economic Stabilization

While the Roosevelt administration was pragmatically trying to pump up the economy, British economist John Maynard Keynes was revolutionizing the way economists viewed government's role in economic policy. Keynes turned conventional economics upside down by arguing four important principles.

First, he demonstrated that conventional economics was wrong in arguing that, in the long run, business cycles tended to leave the economy at "full employment," in which everyone who wanted to work was able to. Keynes argued, "In the long run, we are all dead." In the meantime, the economy would not be at full employment. Instead, it would tend to reach equilibrium at a point below full employment, and a significant number of people who wanted to work would not be able to find jobs.

Second, the reason that the economy would settle at equilibrium below a level of full employment was that overall demand in the economy would not be high enough. Classical economics focused on the behavior of businesses and individuals. Keynes argued that economists instead had to step back and look at the economy as a whole. From that perspective, the level of employment was a product of total demand in the economy. Demand was a function of spending. Left on its own, the economy would not provide enough jobs for everyone who wanted to work. That was because demand would not be high enough. To increase employment, it was necessary to increase demand, and to increase demand required more spending.

Third, Keynes contended that demand in society was a function of spending by individuals, by businesses, and by government. His argument that government played an important role in shaping demand in the economy—and hence in employment—was revolutionary. For the first time, his theory asserted that government played an important role in determining national income and employment.

Fourth, if government played such a role and if the economy were at a level below full employment, the government could pump up economic growth by increasing its spending. That, of course, might well bring a budget deficit. Without governmental "pump priming," however, the economy would stay below full employment. Keynes intended that such deficits would be temporary. Once the economy reached full employment, government budgeting could return to the classical position of balance. And, of course, with a stronger economy the government budget would be far stronger. Under Keynes's theory, a deficit was acceptable if it helped the economy to full employment.

Roosevelt and his advisers thus had stumbled onto precisely what Keynes was suggesting. They launched the New Deal years before the 1936 publication of Keynes's seminal work, *The General Theory of Employment, Internet, and Money*, and Keynes was little known to Roosevelt's key advisers.[4] Together, however, the New Deal and Keynes revolutionized fiscal policy or decision making about the federal budget. Even though the New Deal was thoroughly revolutionary, individuals were going back to work. Keynes's theory provided an intellectual argument for why this was good policy.

Economic historians have long debated whether the New Deal itself ended the Depression. Even at the end of the 1930s, unemployment was still high, and it took the rush to production during World War II to cure the Depression's unemployment. Nevertheless, the lessons of the 1930s were to guide budget makers for generations.

In the process, the norm of budgetary balance slipped from its central place in national economic planning. It is not that everyone did not still seek a solid budgetary policy, or that most people did not see a budgetary balance over time as a test of solidity. Rather, it is that policy makers discovered that they could also use the budget to push the economy to employ as many of the nation's citizens as wanted to work. The policy prescription was clear: The budget should be balanced, not at the level where current revenues equal expenditures, but at the point where the revenues would equal expenditures if the economy were at full employment.

The Rise of Keynesianism

The Keynesian approach to budgetary policy reached its high-water mark during the 1960s. President John Kennedy's economic advisers, Keynesians all, convinced him that the economy was performing below the level of full employment. They told him that a tax cut, even if it increased the deficit in the short run, would spur economic growth, reduce unemployment, and soon yield more tax revenue than the tax cut cost. The proposal bogged down in Congress, but after Kennedy's assassination President Lyndon B. Johnson took up the standard. He saw it as a monument to the fallen president and, not incidentally, as a clear demonstration of his skill in dealing with Congress. Just three months after the assassination, the tax cut was law.[5]

The victory of the Keynesians did not last long. A year later, Johnson began committing substantial American support to the war in Vietnam. This increased spending fueled an already hot economy, and Johnson's advisers began to suggest the need to invoke the other side of the Keynesian equation: a tax increase or a spending cut to slow the boom. If they did not, they fretted, inflation would mount. Federal Reserve Board Chairman William McChesney Martin worried that the boom-bust of the 1920s and 1930s might repeat itself. A consensus emerged among Johnson's economic advisers that the economy would, at some point, have to be slowed. The critical question was when to put on the brakes.

This argument posed a difficult problem for the president. He had no interest in cutting his favorite Great Society programs, and Vietnam meanwhile was demanding ever more spending. A tax increase seemed the better option, but Johnson's advisers were unsure about how much the war would cost and when to impose one. When the administration and the Congress finally agreed on the increase in 1968, it was too little too late. Inflation was rising rapidly, and the administration had lost the chance to leash it before it did serious damage to the economy. To make matters worse, when inflation increased in the early 1970s, the economy did not behave as Keynesian economics predicted. Higher inflation should have brought lower unemployment. During much of the decade, however, the American economy was plagued by simultaneous high inflation *and* high unemployment, a phenomenon christened "stagflation." The fact that economic theory suggested such a thing was impossible failed to console millions of Americans plagued by the loss of their jobs and to the entire nation struggling under the burden of rapidly rising prices, especially for oil. Keynesian economics had no policy prescription for such a situation.

The stagflation of the early 1970s sowed the seeds for the ultimate decline of Keynesianism, but the theory retained a powerful hold on economic policy makers through most of the decade. Even President Richard Nixon, a long-time fiscal conservative, felt compelled to announced his conversion. "I am now a Keynesian," he told one audience. In early 1977, President Jimmy Carter and his advisers considered a tax rebate plan to pump up the economy. Economic growth had slowed, and a Kennedy-style stimulus was needed, they concluded. Before they could convince Congress of the plan, however, inflation reared up once again, and they shelved the proposal.

The Decline of Keynesianism

Keynesian economics quickly lost its power over budgetary policy making. Although in theory it remained an attractive apparatus for understanding the government's role in the economy, it had developed several serious problems in application.

1. Unexplainable stagflation. President Carter's 1977 proposal marked the last time that policy makers would employ the Keynesian apparatus to diagnose policy problems. By the late 1970s, it was clear than Keynesianism in application had developed several important flaws. It could not explain, yet alone solve, the simultaneous high inflation and high unemployment that plagued the American economy during most of the 1970s. It offered solutions to either problem, but it was hamstrung in dealing with both at the same time.

2. Defining full employment. To decide what policy course Keynesianism would suggest in any given situation, budget makers must know whether the economy is at, or below, full employment. Economic statistics are always hard to gather promptly, and even when the numbers are in, "full employment" is hard to gauge. Economic advisers can determine what the unemployment rate is, but they cannot judge for sure at any given point what the level of full employment is. Full employment is not 100 percent. There are always some workers who are between jobs or who otherwise are out of the workforce. Some workers prefer to work part-time or only during some seasons, such as holiday time to earn extra money. Moreover, the level of full employment has changed over time. In the early 1960s, economists estimated that full employment was in the neighborhood of an unemployment rate of 4 percent. By the early 1980s, they guessed it was 5 or perhaps even 6 percent—but no one knew for sure. Without knowing what "full employment" is, policy makers can never be sure which policy prescription to use.

3. Political imbalance. Keynesianism provides a neat and attractive strategy for using the federal budget to make everyone better off. As balanced as the economy theory is, however, it contains a serious political imbalance. Because it is hard to define full employment, it is always attractive to choose the level that allows elected officials to pursue the programs they prefer. Because the definition is fuzzy, it is also hard to know immediately how much pumping is too much. Providing the stimulus to reach full employment is politically an attractive prescription. Few elected officials could resist proposing new spending or lower taxes for such important ends. Which citizen would oppose such appealing choices, especially if they would help the economy? Restraining the economy if growth seems likely to become inflationary, however, is bitter medicine. It is easy for elected officials to postpone taking the pill, and for their advisers to seek more information before deciding that the pill is even necessary. Whatever elegant theoretical symmetry there was in Keynesian economics, there was thus a fatal political asymmetry. So long as it was politically easier to stimulate the economy than to restrain it, the delicate Keynesian balance could never be achieved.

4. *Uncontrollable deficits.* The political imbalance in Keynesianism made it easier to create deficits than to restrain them, and to fuel inflation than to cut it. The theory fueled the appetite for new governmental programs, and policy makers could pursue them eagerly in the belief that they were promoting full employment. The international economic climate worsened the problem, especially during the energy crises during the 1970s. The deficit as a result doubled each decade since World War II through the 1980s.

5. *Less maneuvering room.* The higher the deficit soared, the harder it was to use the budget as an economic tool. Keynesian theory anticipated that the government would not be continually fueling the economy through large deficits. Some Keynesians even suggested that periods of budgetary surplus could slow an overheating economy. However, for a variety of reasons, which we will explore in Chapter 3, the federal deficit moved inexorably upward over time and therefore lost much of its power as an economic tool. It helped worsen the nation's underlying inflation, and once unloosed the inflation proved difficult to cure.

Even though Keynes's theory had much less a hold on policy makers, both the Bush administration and members of Congress quickly grabbed it to respond to the 2001 terrorist attacks. The attacks had wounded the nation, they concluded, and it was their obligation to use the budget to pump up the economy. Political squabbles prevented a timely response, and economists debated about whether budgetary policy really would likely prove an effective tool in stimulating the economy. The debate nevertheless demonstrated that, even though the Keynesian approach had faded from the forefront, it maintained at least a distant hold on policy makers' imaginations. The budget remained closely connected with the economy and elected officials continued to believe—or hope—that their decisions could steer the economy's performance.

Three Stages in Budgeting

The central ideas of federal budgeting thus went through three distinct stages in the nation's first two hundred years. In the first period, from 1789 to 1933, the norm of balance ruled. Even if government officials did not always balance the budget, they always believed that balance was a desirable goal that ought to be met unless some major event, such as war, intervened.

The second period stretched from 1933 to the late 1970s and marked the era of Keynesian economics. The goal of policy makers was to balance the economy, at the point where they could achieve the lowest possible levels of unemployment and inflation, instead of balancing the budget. A deliberately unbalanced budget, in fact, could be desirable under a Keynesian plan to seek full employment. The Keynesian strategy was not a license for unlimited budget deficits, but it did give policy makers a rationale for departing from the norm of budget balance. The ultimate paradox of Keynesianism is that once the idea of a deficit is no longer forbidden, it is hard to restrain its growth. The very logic that established the budget as a tool in steering the national economy in the end made that tool impossible to use.

The third period followed. With the norm of budgetary balance overturned by the New Deal, and Keynesianism capsized by Vietnam war spending and the economic turmoil of stagflation and energy crises in the 1970s, policy makers had no clear guide through the turbulent economy. On what guidance could they rely? Economists produced lots of ideas, but no theory provided an answer with the power of the theories that had crumbled. To make matters worse, two important trends made it harder to make budget decisions. First, the deficit proved stubbornly large and resisted the efforts of Republicans and Democrats, presidents and Congresses, to reduce it. Second, the budget itself changed, leaving decision makers much less discretion. As deficits grew larger, the range of choices grew smaller. It was little wonder that conflict over the federal budget escalated and seeped into nearly every important issue of American politics.

The Debt and the Deficit

The federal debt has grown enormously in the second half of the twentieth century. The total federal debt grew from $257 billion in 1950 to $909 billion in 1980, and then more than quintupled to $6 *trillion* in 2002. These numbers, however, do not necessarily paint an accurate picture of the problem. Unlike family budgets, and even state and local government budgets, the federal budget does not have to be balanced. The federal government can always print more money, if necessary, to finance its deficits. Indeed, since the days of Keynesian economics, experts have argued that running a deficit can be a *good* thing. If government spending were limited to the revenues it took in during wartime, for example, a strong national defense would be impossible when it was most needed. The ability of the federal government to spend in excess of its revenues, and to finance its spending through borrowing, is different from every other budget in the United States.

In fact, the federal debt swelled during World War II, as the nation struggled to pay for a two-front war. As a share of the total economy, the debt gradually shrank until federal deficits in the 1980s sent it upward again. Surpluses in the late 1990s began bringing it back down, until the terrorist attacks of 2001 once again sent the budget back into deficit.

Economists use several different measures to gauge the *size of the deficit*. Everyone begins with the total amount of the debt, expressed in the number of dollars. Over time, however, that measure is less useful. Inflation can reduce the cost of the debt. Meanwhile, the economy grows, so the burden of the debt— its total value and the costs of paying annual interest—can shrink. So economists compare the size of the debt to the size of the economy to get a sense of its overall burden. Thus, Figure 2–1 charts the total number of dollars and the better measure, the debt as a percentage of the gross domestic product (GDP)— the total of goods and services produced in the domestic economy, which is the standard measure of the size of the economy. We'll use the GDP in other comparisons in this book for the same reason.

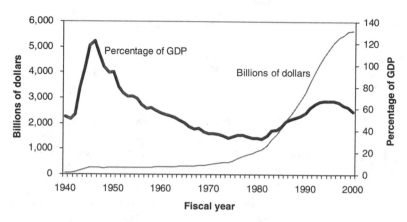

Figure 2–1   Federal Debt

Source: Office of Management and Budget, *Budget of the United States Government: Fiscal Year 2002, Historical Tables* (Washington, D.C.: Government Printing Office, 2001).

It is one thing to chart changes in the debt over time. It is another to forecast the size of the debt in the future. The more money that economists forecast the economy will make available—and the less money the government consumes—the more room there is for policy makers to craft their decisions. They can choose to reduce the debt, or they can use extra money to cut taxes or increase spending.

That is just what happened in 2001. Early in the year, the Congressional Budget Office (CBO, Congress's nonpartisan forecasters) estimated a ten-year budget surplus of $5.61 trillion. That immediately led to a debate over what to do with it. President Bush and Republican members of Congress argued that it ought to be used in part for a tax cut and in part to reduce the debt. Democratic members of Congress argued for a smaller tax cut and a fix for social security's finances. By August, unemployment had risen substantially and CBO's forecast projected only a $3.39 trillion surplus. Two months later, the congressional budget committees estimated that the surplus would be just $2.60 billion. By January 2002, CBO estimated that the ten-year surplus would be just $1.6 trillion, a drop of $4 trillion—almost three-fourths—in just one year.[6] Of the

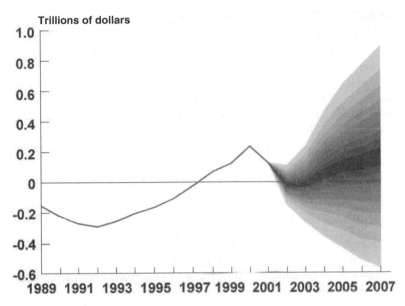

Figure 2–2   Uncertainty in Budget Projections
Source: Congressional Budget Office.

decline, 60 percent came from legislative decisions (tax cuts and more spending); 40 percent came from the weakening economy.

CBO's new estimates stunned policy makers and analysts alike. In just a year, the debate had switched to the dilemma of figuring out how to deal with a huge and growing surplus to the evaporation of the surplus and the possibility of a new growth in federal debt. In fact, CBO frankly admitted that the further out its projections went, the most uncertain it was about what was going to happen. In January 2002, for example, CBO estimated that its forecast six years into the future could be for a surplus as large as $1 trillion—or a deficit as large as $600 billion. As Figure 2–2 shows, the further into the future the projections went, the less certain CBO was.

These facts reveal two central truths about budgeting and the federal debt. One lies in looking to the past: The debt has meaning only in comparison with the size of the economy. Sheer numbers can sound impressive, but their historical significance lies in their size relative to the economy and its growth. The other lies in looking to the future: The further into the future analysts look into their crystal ball, the fuzzier their vision becomes. That provides a weak guide in advance as policy makers frame their decisions. Indeed, the real meaning of their decisions often only becomes clear years later. The uncertainty makes the basic differences in political values all the more important as elected officials decide. When the future is cloudy and conflict is high, values rule.

As the size of the debt shifts, two questions are fundamental: If the government has to borrow money to finance its spending, who lends it the money? And how much borrowing is too much?

Who Owns the Federal Government's Debt?

A look at who actually owns the federal debt reveals some surprises. The first surprise is that the government itself owns about 40 percent of the debt. Several important government programs, including highway construction, airport construction, military and civilian retirement, Medicare, and social security, are financed through trust funds. Revenues come into these funds from earmarked sources, such as the fees collected from the sale of each gallon of gas (for the highway trust fund) or the purchase of a ticket (for the airline trust fund). When the trust fund runs a surplus (that is, when it takes in more money than it spends), federal law requires that these surpluses be invested in federal securities.

A second large piece of the federal debt—9 percent in 2000— is held by the Federal Reserve. The Fed, as it is popularly known, manages the nation's money supply and affects the level of interest rates. The Fed uses its large holding of Treasury securities to conduct what are called "open-market operations." When it wants to put more money into circulation, it buys Treasury securities from other investors, thus trading the investors' securities for cash. When it wants to take money out of circulation, it sells Treasury securities, thus trading cash for securities. Putting money into circulation generally helps bring interest rates down, and taking money out of circulation helps drive interest rates up. Any money that the Fed makes on its operations, in addition to its costs, is returned to the Treasury.

Of the debt held by the public, most consists of investments by Americans seeking a safe and secure investment. Banks hold a substantial part of this debt along with individuals, especially through savings bonds and mutual funds. State and local governments find Treasury securities attractive investments for their pension plans for retired government workers. Foreign financiers likewise see the national debt as one of the world's most risk-free investments. The federal government's debt is the gold standard of securities. Investors widely believe that it is the safest investment in the world, and the federal government's long-term debt has become the benchmark to which investment managers peg their interest rates.

Thus, the most gruesome fears usually raised about the federal debt are unfounded. The federal deficit is not being funded by money spewing from printing presses. Instead, it is financed mainly by Americans themselves, who seek a safe investment for their money. Big surpluses in government trust funds are paying for a large part of the rest. The federal government rarely has any trouble selling its debt. If the federal government is not good for the money, investors ask, who else could be?

Why Do the Debt and Deficit Matter?

The real question, however, is not *whether* the debt can be sold but *how much* it costs to do so. The debt burden, measured as a share of the economy, gradually diminished after World War II. The debt grew, but the economy grew much more quickly. By 1975, the national debt was less than one third as large (measured as a share of the gross domestic product) as it was in 1945. Soon afterward, however, the deficit began to grow quickly, and the national debt increased much more quickly than the economy. The *real* costs of the debt and the deficit rose likewise.

Economists have long argued about just how important these costs are. Some argue that the continued high deficits, especially those during the 1980s, are disastrous, while others argue that they pose little danger. Charles L. Schultze, chairman of the president's Council of Economic Advisers during the Carter administration, characterizes economists' approach to the effects of the deficit in three ways.[7]

Some economists look on the deficit as a _domesticated pussycat_. They contend that the deficit is greatly overrated as a problem and argue that, especially after taking account of inflation, surpluses in state and local budgets, and investments in long-term projects such as highways and waste treatment facilities, the deficit is trivial. Among these pussycats are some very conservative economists who seek to defend the Reagan administration's economic record, despite the high deficits that resulted. Others are liberals who view the size of the deficit as small as they seek to make the case for more government spending. The numbers of both groups are small, however, and support for their position is slight.

The second group of economists looks on the deficit as _a wolf at the door_. These economists foresee an eventual crisis because of the persistent deficits. Investors, especially from abroad, the wolves argue, might lose confidence in the American economy because policy makers seem incapable of managing the federal budget. The more investors lose confidence, the less likely they would be to hold American dollars, and the value of the dollar would therefore drop. Inflation and interest rates in the United States would soar. A stock market crash and a deep recession would follow. Many economists, including domestic and international business analysts, held this view at the beginning of the 1980s. The higher the deficits rose and the longer the nation went without the feared economic collapse, however, the weaker the wolves' position became.

The final group of economists sees the deficit as _termites in the basement_. The great problem with termites is that they work quietly, without notice, for years, until they ruin the foundation and risk collapsing the house. That, Schultze and most other leading economists argue, is the problem with the deficit. It may not be the most critical problem facing policy makers, but bit by bit it is eroding the quality of life in the United States.

The Deficit and Investment

Directly connected with rising deficits is a pair of problems. Americans have for decades proven to be poor savers. On the other hand, American consumption—from housing to food to clothes and cars—has at the same time risen to historically high levels. With

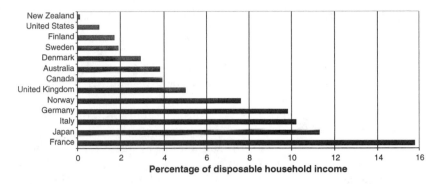

Figure 2–3   Household Savings Rate in 2000

Source: Organization for Economic Cooperation and Development.

investment low and consumption high, "the nation as a whole has been living beyond its means," the General Accounting Office, Congress's audit agency, has argued.[8] As economist Benjamin M. Friedman puts it, "America has thrown itself a party and billed the tab to the future. The costs, which are only beginning to come due, will include a lower standard of living for individual Americans and reduced American influence and importance in world affairs."[9]

As the deficit has risen, the American savings rate has shrunk, from about 9 percent in the 1960s and 1970s to 3.7 percent from 1980 to 1987. By 2000, the savings rate was just 1 percent. Savings in the United States has fallen to a fraction of the rate in many of the world's other industrial nations (see Figure 2–3). As the General Accounting Office continued in its analysis, "With the economy running close to full capacity, large and persistent budget deficits undermine the future well-being of the country by consuming savings that would otherwise be available to finance investment supporting long-term economic growth." Simply put, "those who grow are those who save."

Moreover, the size of the debt squeezes the federal budget. Each year, federal policy makers must pay interest on the debt, much as homeowners must make regular payments on the their mortgages. During the 1980s, in fact, interest on the debt was one of the most quickly growing federal programs, rising from 8.5 percent of federal spending in 1979 to 14.8 percent in 1989. By 2000, the burden had shrank to 12.5 percent of total spending, but the prospect of rising deficits once again threatened to send interest payments higher.

Why does this matter? Every dollar spent on interest on the national debt is a dollar that cannot be spent on another program. When interest payments increase, they squeeze out other possible uses of the government's money. Housing programs, college aid, food for the poor, health research, defense programs—all are under much greater pressure when the burden of paying interest on the national debt pinches the budget.

Foreigners helped finance a large part of the increase in the national debt. Interest payments made to foreigners increased rapidly as a result. In 1970, the federal government paid $1 billion in interest to foreigners. By 1989, the total was $33.4 billion. From just 1985 to 1989, interest payments to foreigners increased by almost 12 percent per year.[10] On one level, this change is attractive, since we have been able to finance domestic consumption by borrowing from others. On a more important level, however, this increase poses real dangers. A growing portion of American tax revenues are going abroad to pay foreigners who are lending us money. The United States, as a result, has become a debtor nation to the rest of the world. Although it is attractive to have someone else help pay the bills, the rise in consumption and decline in savings worsens the nation's two other major deficits, the deficit in its international trade and its deficit in domestic investment.

INTERNATIONAL TRADE.   As American consumption has risen, it has grown faster than the nation's ability to produce. As a result, imports from abroad have increased rapidly, from cars and televisions to a wide variety of clothing and other consumer goods. On the whole, we have tended to buy more from abroad than foreigners have bought from us. The result is an enormous trade deficit, in which our imports greatly exceed our exports. For consumers, the trade deficit has had an attractive side. The quality of goods available for purchase has been high and the price has been right. For the economy as a whole, however, the sustained trade deficit of the 1980s has had serious consequences. The larger the imbalance of trade— as we import more than we export—the more we export jobs. When on balance we buy more from abroad than we sell there, the more our consumption finances the expansion of employment abroad at the expense of employment at home.

DOMESTIC INVESTMENT. The imbalance of trade is coupled directly with low domestic investment. Keeping American industries competitive requires investment for the future in new products, new methods of manufacturing, new equipment, and new skills for workers. The more we consume, the less we invest, and the less we invest the more we lose ground with our international competitors. Workers must use older equipment, work less efficiently, and produce fewer goods of lower quality. Productivity lags and wage increases may fail to match inflation. Since World War II, the wages earned by American workers, even after accounting for inflation, steadily rose. In the mid-1970s, however, the growth ended and by 1989, wages (after accounting for inflation) were lower than in the level twenty years before.[11]

The party now, pay-later approach promises significant problems for the future. Low rates of investment mean that we are not building the facilities and equipment we will need for future economic growth. In just one area of the economy, the nation's transportation system, this means that the nation's roads, bridges, mass-transit systems, and airports are gradually deteriorating. If investments are not made in the present to deal with future problems, gridlock will inevitably grow. The General Accounting Office estimates that, by 2005, urban traffic congestion will grow 300 percent. The congestion will waste 7.3 billion gallons of fuel per year, and users will face a $50 billion per year bill just for the fuel. Instead of making these investments, however, money is being spent for current consumption.[12]

The problem extends past the problem of transportation, which is certainly bad enough, to the future living standards of today's workers. Once upon a time, "It was expected that each generation of Americans would live better than the last with hard work and perseverance," analyst Richard C. Michel pointed out. "It's just not true any more." For example, almost two thirds of young American families have dual incomes. The number of working wives in the economy has expanded enormously since the 1970s, and the workforce has changed dramatically. The huge increase in the number of working wives, however, has helped family income barely stay even, for family income is now about the same as it was in the 1950s and 1960s, when just one income supported the family. Monthly mortgage payments on a median-priced family home cost about 15 percent of family income in the 1950s and 1960s. By the early 1990s, the share had doubled to 30 percent.[13]

Families were working harder but were barely keeping even. Projections by some analysts suggested that the situation would be even worse for today's college students. Without investing for the future, the American tradition of an upwardly mobile society cannot continue. The interest rates that Americans will have to pay to finance cars, homes, and new industry will be high, wages will decline, and the American standard of living will decay. It would be an exaggeration to suggest that all of these problems stem directly from the deficit. The deficit, however, undoubtedly is a major contributor to the problems. Curing the problems, furthermore, is impossible without higher national savings, and increasing savings is very difficult when the deficit is high. The overwhelming consensus of economists and financial analysts is that persistent deficits are dangerous. As *New York Times* columnist Tom Wicker argued, "If you want safe bridges, a decent environment and a host of other desirable physical and social effects—a better educated work force, for instance, and a lower child mortality rate—then the government needs to invest more, not less, in American society."[14] The consensus is that the deficit must be brought down. The problem is that the uncertainties in budget forecasting make it hard to be sure how much money is available to spend without swelling the debt further—and that fundamental disagreements on whether to cut taxes or increase spending always lie at the core of budget battles.

What Should We Balance?

In the heat of budgetary battles, it is easy to get so caught up in the deficit numbers that we miss the most fundamental questions. Nearly everyone agrees that the deficit must be reduced. Few careful observers, however, argue that the deficit needs to be reduced to zero.

How much of a deficit is too much? How do know when we have reduced the deficit enough?

Most economists contend that we should not seek to balance the budget, even if it were politically possible. To cut spending or raise taxes enough to bring the deficit to zero, they argue persuasively, would wreck the economy. In seeking an arbitrary match of revenues and expenditures, the federal government would be slowing economic growth and redistributing income in ways that might not be desirable. Furthermore, as Herbert Stein, chairman of the Council of Economic Advisers in the Nixon and Ford administrations, contends, "Balancing the budget is not the name of the game. The name of the game is making good use of the national output, which may or not involve balancing the budget."[15] A balanced budget has a certain appeal to tidiness, but there is no reason that balance must be an end in itself.

Why do governments budget? They do so to make fundamental decisions on how the nation's wealth ought to be spent. On behalf of us all, governments shift resources from private to public uses, such as national defense. They shift resources from rich to poor, from young to old, from cities to rural areas or vice versa, or among regions of the country. They shape decisions about how much of the nation's wealth we enjoy now versus how much we ought to invest for the future. Seen in this broader perspective, the budget deficit is the result of other, much more complex decisions. It is an artifact of spending policies, tax strategies, and overall economic growth. To focus solely on the deficit is to miss these larger, and ultimately more important, questions.

In the end, the real problem is not balancing the budget but budgeting the nation's wealth, Stein perceptively contends.[16] Seen through this lens, the fundamental question is not whether we have a deficit but, rather, what underlying decisions the deficit represents. Are we spending too much in some areas that are less productive than in others that might promote our common goals better? Do we tax in ways that distort the way the economy operates? Does a consistent and large deficit have serious implications for the future, especially since it means we consume now instead of investing for the future? Stein contends that "current budget processes are not allocating the national output well."[17]

Thus, we have had a persistent deficit and budget problems. The problem, however, is not that the budget has arithmetically been out of balance. The real problems, rather, are three. First, the battles are signs that we are not making the best use of the nation's wealth. Important problems go unsolved, while we spend much money on programs that do not substantially improve our circumstances. Second, the persistent battles undercut our chances for long-term economic growth. The short-term problems may not seem serious, but the effects on our children and grandchildren could well be substantial. Finally, the deficit issue itself, with all its symbolism and rhetoric, has become both cause and effect of ongoing problems of governance. Important decisions on the budget tend to be ducked or not made at all, while other critical policy issues become casualties to the budget wars.

Everyone, therefore, believes that the deficit must be brought down—not for its own sake, but because of the effects that large and sustained deficits produce for both the economy and the political system. What choices are there for doing so? We turn to this question in Chapter 3.

Notes

1. For an interesting look at the norms of public budgeting, see Aaron Wildavsky, *The New Politics of the Budgetary Process* (Glenview, Ill.: Scott, Foresman/Little Brown, 1988), pp. 397–402.
2. See Herbert Stein, *The Fiscal Revolution in America* (Chicago: University of Chicago Press, 1969), pp. 3–16.
3. Marriner S. Eccles, *Beckoning Frontiers: Public and Personal Recollections* (New York: Alfred A. Knopf, 1951). For a discussion, see pp. 129–31, 79–81.
4. John Maynard Keynes, *The General Theory of Employment, Interest, and Money* (New York: Harcourt, Brace, 1936).
5. A more detailed study of the rise and fall of Keynesianism during the Johnson years can be found in Donald F. Kettl, "The Economic Education of Lyndon Johnson: Guns, Butter, and Taxes," in *The Johnson Years, Volume II: Vietnam, the Environment, and Science,* ed. Robert A. Divine (Lawrence: University Press of Kansas, 1987), pp. 54–78.

6. Statement of Dan L. Crippen, Director, Congressional Budget Office, "The Budget and Economic Outlook: Fiscal Years 2003–2012," before the Committee on the Budget, U.S. House of Representatives (January 23, 2002); and estimates compiled by Richard W. Stevenson, "Huge Decline Seen in Budget Surplus over Next Decade," *New York Times*, January 6, 2002, Sec. 1, p. 19.

7. Quoted in David E. Rosenbaum, "Why the Deficit is Paralyzing Congress," *New York Times*, October 22, 1989, Sec. 4, p. 1.

8. U.S. General Accounting Office, *Budget Deficit: Appendixes on Outlook, Implications, and Choices* (Washington, D.C.: Government Printing Office, 1990), pp. 8–9.

9. Quoted in ibid., p. 3.

10. GAO, *Budget Deficit*, p. 10.

11. GAO, *Budget Deficit*, pp. 52–53.

12. Kirk Victor, "Paying for the Roads," *National Journal* 23 (February 16, 1991), pp. 374–9.

13. "Boomers' Old Age May Be Bleak," [Madison, Wis.] *Capital Times*, February 19, 1991, pp. 3A, 3D. More generally, see Frank Levy and Richard C. Michel, *The Economic Future of American Families* (Washington, D.C.: Urban Institute Press, 1991).

14. *New York Times*, November 7, 1990, p. A21.

15. Herbert Stein, *Governing the $5 Trillion Economy* (New York: Oxford University Press, 1989), p. 2.

16. Ibid., p. 7.

17. Ibid., p. 10.

CHAPTER 3

Tough Choices

Arguments on the budget, from virtually every perspective, lead to the same conclusion. Nearly everyone agrees that the budget ought to be balanced. But if everyone agrees on the goal, why have elected officials not done a better job of accomplishing it? The simple answer is that there are no easy choices. Any budgetary decision that makes a real difference inevitably hurts someone and generates enormous conflict. Furthermore, as budget makers struggle to make these decisions, they discover that the very structure of the budget has changed in ways that greatly limit their choices.

Budget battles are not the result of obstinate decision makers forming perverse decisions. They are, rather, the result of well-meaning men and women wrestling with questions that yield no easy answers. Even as Americans have struggled to limit government's power, we have long demanded much from government. We expect a strong national defense to prevent foreign enemies from interfering with our lives. We want easy, safe transportation, and we expect decent shelter. We require safe drinking water and clean air. We want to be secure in our old age and to have quality education for our children. On top of that, we dislike taxes, especially for programs whose benefits we cannot easily see. The old maxim, "Don't tax you. Don't tax me. Tax that man behind the tree" guides much of our fiscal policy. We expect much but are reluctant to empower government to give it to us. We are especially reluctant to yield to government any more than the minimum authority to tax us for the goods and services we want.

There are as many different answers to the deficit puzzle as there are participants in the political process. Any approach to the deficit, and federal budgeting more generally, however, hinges on three basic questions:

1. How much should we spend on national defense versus domestic programs?
2. In domestic programs, how much should we spend on entitlement programs, such as social security and medicare, versus discretionary programs, such as education and job training?
3. How should we raise the money we spend?

Defense Versus Domestic Programs

Arguments over guns versus butter, defense versus domestic programs, are as old as the nation. George Washington struggled constantly to extract funds from a reluctant Continental Congress to finance the war for independence, and things have changed little since. Americans expect to be free from foreign domination, and we take for granted the fact that no war with a foreign power has ever been fought on American soil. At the same, Americans have always been reluctant to maintain a standing military and have been suspicious of those who profit from the military's business. In President Eisenhower's farewell address, he warned of a military-industrial complex that would demand a huge share of America's wealth to perpetuate its power. How much defense is enough? What kind of defense should it be? And at what point does the search for a strong defense run headlong into domestic needs?

The Growth of Defense Spending

Defense politics has long been locked in distinctive Republican-versus-Democrat differences. Republicans have postured themselves as strong on defense and have accused Democrats of weakening national security. Democrats counter that Republicans have been too eager to increase defense spending, often without planning the expenditures well and without asking whether domestic programs might need the money more. Since World War II, however, the

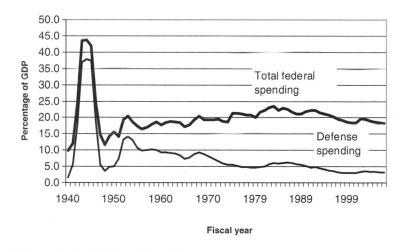

Figure 3–1   Defense Spending

Source: Office of Management and Budget, *Budget of the United States Government, Fiscal Year 2003: Historical Tables* (GPO, 2002), Table 6–1.

pattern of spending among Democratic and Republican presidents does not support the conventional wisdom. As Figure 3–1 shows, defense expenditures declined in the early 1960s until the Vietnam War. Defense spending started declining in the succeeding Republican administrations, under Presidents Nixon and Ford, as Vietnam War costs ended. As a presidential candidate, Ronald Reagan claimed that Democratic president Jimmy Carter was weak on defense, but defense spending actually started rising in the second half of the Carter administration, restoring spending that had been cut during Republican presidencies. The Reagan defense buildup accelerated the increase, but only until fiscal year 1986, when defense spending began declining again (when measured as a share of the national economy)—until the Bush administration's response to the September 11, 2001, terrorist attacks led to proposals to increase it again.

We can draw three conclusions from these trends. First, although there have been strong partisan squabbles on defense policy, especially within Congress and between Congress and the president, defense spending does not show a partisan pattern at the presidential level. Bigger issues, including wars and the nation's international situation, have shaped defense spending instead. Second, since the mid-1970s, the overall level of defense spending has been relatively flat. If anything, it has gradually diminished as a share of the economy. The Reagan defense buildup was substantial, but even at its high point it was below the level of the pre–Vietnam War 1960s. Third, domestic spending has increased far more rapidly than spending for national defense. Its increase began almost precisely at the same time, in the early 1970s, that defense spending began shrinking. We will return shortly to the domestic issues, but for now we can note that the usual guns-versus-butter debate, of defense versus domestic programs, misses important changes over time.

The Reagan defense buildup is important for other reasons, however. Previous increases in defense spending occurred during wartime. In the Reagan years, the increases followed the Reagan administration's contentions that American military preparedness had dropped to a dangerously low level and that only by bargaining from strength could the nation hope to face down its foes, especially the Soviet Union. Such increases in peacetime had no precedent. Nearly all of the new spending, furthermore, went not into increasing the size of the armed forces but into building expensive and complicated weapons systems. Some of these systems were ambitious new programs, such as the radar-evading B-2 stealth bomber and the Strategic Defense Initiative, the "Star Wars" space-based system designed to knock out incoming nuclear warheads. Some of the money also went toward expansion of existing weapons, such as the goal of building a 600-ship navy.

By the mid-1980s, however, Congress stopped the buildup. With the budget deficit soaring and important domestic needs going unmet, members of Congress argued that the nation could no longer afford the Reagan administration's ambitious plans. By the early 1990s, the breakdown of communism in eastern Europe and serious domestic problems in the Soviet Union removed, virtually overnight the threat against which the United States had been preparing for forty years. Critics of the Reagan administration's legacy argued that the money could be better spent elsewhere in the budget.

The Clinton administration held the line on defense spending, but President Bush argued that the nation had no alternative but to strengthen defense in the aftermath of the terrorist attacks. He proposed a larger budget to fund "a plan to fight a war we did not seek—but a war we are determined to win." He proposed, in fact "the biggest increase in defense spending in 20 years, to pay the cost of war and the price of transforming our Cold War military into a new twenty-first century fighting force."[1] Defense policy—and defense spending—shifted in response to outside threats and the president's ability to build a consensus behind his view of how the nation could best respond.

New Strategies for Changing Problems

Critics of the Reagan administration's defense plans argued that the defense budget had to be both lower and smarter. The disintegration of the Soviet threat, coupled with the lessons taught by the war with Iraq, dramatically changed American defense plans in the early 1990s. Soviet troops were withdrawn from countries that used to lie behind what was once called the iron curtain. The major physical piece of that curtain, the Berlin Wall, was dismantled, and many Soviet-bloc countries held free elections. Within the Soviet Union, ethnic minorities pressed for more voice in their own governance, and the entire nation struggled with critical shortages of virtually every important good.

After forty years of building a heavily-armed ground-based force in Europe and a massive nuclear retaliatory force around the world, the Pentagon virtually overnight had to redefine its future mission. Then, as Americans celebrated their victory in the Cold War against the Soviets and President Bush announced a "new world order," war with Iraq erupted. The war demonstrated the need to be able to project substantial military force thousands of miles on short notice. The problems facing the national defense were suddenly dramatically different, and the new problems demanded new strategies and tactics.

The core of the revised plans devised by American military planners was a new diagnosis of future needs. Instead of preparing for a massive battle in defense against aggressive Soviet forces, they instead developed new strategies for quick offensive action in wars like the one against Iraq. Anticipating that small skirmishes and major challenges might pop up anywhere around the world, Pentagon planners drew up plans for a rapid-deployment force, whose air, land, and sea elements could be intermixed as needed. As one of these planners put it, "Never in the foreseeable future are we going to have a 1987-sized army." The new question is, how do we fight smart?[2] In the aftermath of wars in Iraq and Afghanistan, a widespread debate emerged about how to position the military for the challenges of the twenty-first century.

The new strategy of fighting smart carries three implications, which mark strong departures from the Reagan administration buildup.[3] First, in part because of domestic political realities and in part because of changing international conditions, deep cuts in the Pentagon's conventional force structure were inevitable. By fiscal year 1995, for example, Pentagon planners estimated that the number of active army divisions would be cut from eighteen to twelve, and that reserve army divisions would decrease from ten to six. The number of navy combat ships would fall by one fourth, and the air force would retire 400 fighters and bombers. Even the Pentagon civilian workforce was expected to be reduced by nearly 100,000 employees, 10 percent of the total. Conventional forces, which had formed the core of the American military since World War II, would see big reductions.

The second implication is an increase in support for rapid-deployment and forces for regional wars around the world. The navy, for example, was expected to buy more transport ships, after discovering in the war against Iraq that it was not well-equipped for quickly moving forces to the Middle East. The air force, which had planned to end production of the ungainly "Warthog," the A-10 attack plane that proved effective against Iraqi tanks, would keep the plane in its lineup. The renewed importance of both systems was ironic, because neither branch had liked either system much in the past. The navy had long pressed aircraft carriers as the centerpiece of its forces, as an ideal way to project sophisticated forces long distances. Operating a seaborne trucking service was not nearly as attractive. The air force, for its part, had opposed systems for close support of ground forces. Its leaders preferred instead the high-tech long-range bombers, such as the B-1 and the radar-evading B-2, and sophisticated high-speed fighters for air battles. The big buildup of the 1980s had focused especially on the air force and navy, and now both branches found they had to reconsider missions they had long resisted.

The third implication is the expansion of high-tech weapons. Americans were mesmerized in the first days of the 1991 war against Iraq by television pictures showing cruise missiles moving down the streets of Baghdad, "smart bombs" that went right through the doors of hardened shelters, and Patriot missiles blowing Iraqi Scud missiles out of the sky. In the war in Afghanistan, unpiloted drones proved especially effective in minimizing the exposure of American troops while providing high-quality intelligence about the movement of enemy troops. These weapons demonstrated enormous potential for increasing the effectiveness of the armed forces and minimizing the losses of American forces. The Pentagon thus found itself moving simultaneously in opposite directions. Expansion of relatively unsexy transport and support equipment came hand-in-hand with new weapons enhanced with sophisticated electronics. This paradoxical low-tech/high-tech strategy was to shape American military spending into the 1990s.

Implications for the Budget

Under the budget's pressures, some of the armed services' favorite weapons systems were canceled. Just a week before the outbreak of war with Iraq in January 1991, for example, Defense Secretary Richard Cheney (before he served as vice president) terminated the navy's advanced, radar-evading A-12 bomber after the nation had invested $3.1 billion in the plane. Cost overruns and performance problems had plagued the bomber, and Cheney concluded that the defense budget's coming lean years did not allow for taking chances with such a risky system. Other projects that had grown out of the 1980s, such as the Strategic Defense Initiative and the B-2 bomber, suffered heavy cuts. Defense programs that grew out of the Pentagon's $35 billion "black budget," the secret part of the defense budget hiding highly classified projects, were especially vulnerable.

Budgeters who sought to cut the defense budget, however, rediscovered a critical problem about defense spending. Adjusting the defense budget is like steering a supertanker: It takes a long time after turning the wheel to change direction. Today's defense spending is the result of decisions made years ago. Officials in the Pentagon cannot simply order a new bomber or an aircraft carrier from a manufacturer. Instead, they must design the weapon, negotiate a contract, and agree on a schedule for delivery. This process takes a very long time—often from five to eight years. Fulfilling these orders requires huge investments by the manufacturers, who naturally seek to protect themselves by building high cancellation penalties into the contracts. The government therefore can rarely realize immediate savings by ending a project immediately.

Today's defense spending is thus the result of contracts negotiated years ago. Similarly, today's budget decisions will take years to show up in federal spending. These factors create perverse incentives for budget makers. It is very hard to do anything that produces quick budget savings. Years often roll by before significant budget savings emerge from decisions, and in the meantime budget makers have had to go through politically painful battles over closing bases or canceling contracts. The very structure of the defense budget, therefore, makes it difficult to fight wrenching battles today for savings that materialize only slowly. The defense budget thus is frustrating for those who seek to change it.

Discretionary Versus Entitlement Programs

The seemingly endless skirmishes over defense versus domestic spending have camouflaged the fact that, since the early 1960s, domestic spending has grown by more than 50 percent while defense spending has shrunk by nearly 50 percent. This scarcely fits the conventional wisdom. Why are there such defense-versus–domestic policy battles if domestic spending has grown so quickly? Is it a clever tactic by those seeking to increase domestic spending even more quickly? Or is there something else going on?

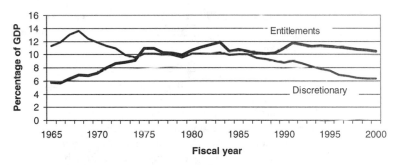

Figure 3-2   Discretionary Versus Entitlement Spending

Source: Congressional Budget Office, *The Budget and Economic Outlook: Fiscal Years 2002–2011* (Washington, D.C.: GPO, January 2001), Table 9.

The answer is the latter, because domestic spending consists of two very different pieces. Spending for *discretionary programs*, that is, programs over which Congress has year-to-year control, has risen and fallen with presidential initiatives, as Figure 3–2 shows. During the 1970s, new intergovernmental block grant programs for community development and job training, for example, swelled discretionary domestic spending. During the 1980s, the Reagan administration squeezed these programs and other domestic programs, from community health clinics and criminal justice to air-traffic control and legal aid. By 2000, spending for discretionary domestic programs was about half of what it had been in the early 1960s, when measured as a percentage of the GNP.

Spending for *entitlement programs* is a far different story. Entitlement programs are those in which the government is required by law to make payments, usually payment to individuals, to anyone who meets the law's criteria. For example, anyone who meets the social security law's basic standards (retiring at age 62 with a minimum number of years of service, among other guidelines) is entitled to a monthly check, with the amount defined by law. Other major entitlement programs include medicare, which provides medical care for the elderly; farm price supports, which provide payments to farmers producing certain products, such as milk; and civilian and military retirement programs, which distribute monthly checks to retirees. Measured as a share of the GNP, spending for entitlements almost doubled from 1962 through 2000. Entitlement debates, moreover, have taken on an old-versus-young picture, since about 60 percent of all entitlement spending goes for the elderly.

Entitlements are payments made by the government to individuals who meet requirements in law. Some individuals are entitled to payments because of their age, in the social security and medicare programs, for example. Some individuals are entitled to payments because of their income, in the welfare and medicaid programs. Some individuals are entitled to payments because they share a condition, such as having been victims of a natural disaster. The key things about entitlement programs are that the government spends the money automatically and that individuals can receive the payments automatically.

It is no exaggeration to say that entitlement spending has been the major engine driving federal spending upward since the 1960s. Entitlement spending has grown much faster than the growth in total spending, and it now accounts for *half all federal spending*. A series of subtle, sometimes barely noticed, policy changes has steadily and gradually pushed entitlement spending up as other spending has been squeezed down. As tempting as it might be to play partisan games with the issue of federal spending, the fact is that the growth of federal spending is not fueled by free-spending Democrats, as Republicans such as Ronald Reagan often charge. Indeed, the Reagan administration's struggle to cut domestic spending made only a temporary dent in entitlement spending before it resumed its upward course. Instead, spending growth has been driven by entitlements, and that entitlement spending has both Republican and Democratic fingerprints on it.

Social Security

The most important of the federal entitlement programs is social security, which dates from the Social Security Act of 1935. Proponents sold the new social security program to voters as an insurance program. Individuals would contribute a portion of their paychecks, and their contributions would be totaled in their own names in special accounts. When retirement (or a few other circumstances) arrived, the government would send a monthly check, with the amount calculated based on the recipient's contributions and final salary. With such a foundation, it is little wonder that social security has nearly sacred status among all federal programs. Workers look on it as an explicit contract with the government, and any attempt to change it is invariably seen as a breach of faith.

Social security, however, never was an insurance program. From its first days, it has been a pay-as-you-go program financed by a special payroll tax. When the federal government created the medicare program—the nation's health and hospital insurance program for senior citizens—it was financed in the same way. Policy makers have long nourished the idea that workers' contributions go into a special account earmarked to pay for their benefits later in life. That has an obvious attraction. If workers simply get their own money back, then it is politically very hard to reduce the program. In fact, however, the taxes of today's workers have always been used to pay for the benefits of today's workers. That was inevitable because the government made retired workers eligible for both social security and medicare as soon as the programs were created, and most recipients got back far more than they had paid in.

Social security and medicare are financed by a *payroll tax*—a tax on the money earned by workers. To fund the programs, the federal government taxes earnings at 7.65 percent (6.2 percent for social security and 1.45 percent for medicare). Employers match the employees' contributions. Economists have long argued that employees effectively pay the employers' share: Employers pay lower wages to make up for the payroll tax they must pay.

The 1983 Rescue

By the 1980s, however, the program began experiencing serious problems. The government began paying out more money than it was taking in, and that created deficits in the program. To stem the flow of red ink, the Reagan administration in 1981 proposed reducing social security benefits for persons retiring before age 65, tightening eligibility requirements for the program, and reducing cost-of-living increases.

Senior citizens responded furiously and handed President Reagan the worst defeat of his administration. Seniors flooded their members of Congress with letters, telegrams, and telephone calls in protest. The head of one lobbying group for senior citizens said, "Old people are being thrown to the sharks."[4] When the plan died, the administration followed the ageless Washington strategy of naming a study commission to solve the problem. The commission, headed by the former Council of Economic Advisers chairman and, later, the Federal Reserve Board chairman, Alan Greenspan, produced a plan that served as the model for a 1983 reform of the entire social security system. Congress and the president agreed to increase the retirement age gradually to age 67 (by the year 2022); to expand social security coverage to new federal employees and workers in nonprofit organizations (which brought in substantial immediate revenue while delaying increased costs until they retired); a different formula that produced slightly lower cost-of-living increases; and substantially higher payroll taxes for workers.

The Reagan administration's early political debacle on social security firmly established a political principle. Republicans could not suggest reducing entitlements, for then they would be viewed as the party that wanted to hurt the elderly. Having gained the upper hand, Democrats struggled to avoid anything that would tarnish their image of creators and defenders of the program. As a result, social security became virtually untouchable. The idea of asking whether it had a higher priority for government taxes became ever more unthinkable.

Meanwhile, a largely unnoticed accounting change included in the 1983 social security rescue insulated the social security program even further. One central idea behind the rescue was to accumulate a large pool of savings late in the twentieth century and early in the twenty-first century to help fund retirement payments for the huge number of baby boomers, born in the late 1940s and in the 1950s. The idea was to run a substantial surplus in the social security program and to invest the money for the future. The government cannot literally save money for the future, of course. It can buy

Treasury securities, which reduces the amount of obligations that the Treasury must sell elsewhere to finance the national debt. Private investors would then look to the private sector for investing their money, and the investments they made would help fuel economic growth. A stronger economy when the baby boomers retired would thus help finance their social security payments. That, in turn, would help lessen the burden on future workers, because demographers projected that there would be even fewer workers per social security recipient in the future than now.

To keep track of the projected surplus in social security, the 1983 rescue took the social security program "off-budget." That is, while the revenue it collected and the payments it made would be counted in calculating overall government statistics, including the deficit, it would not otherwise be part of the annual budgetary process. The growing surplus, however, soon had an unexpected effect on deficit politics.

From an $11 billion deficit in fiscal 1983, the balance in the social security trust fund grew to $152 billion in 2000. For most of that period, the rest of the budget was in deficit and the federal government's spending in response to the 2001 terrorist attacks put the rest of the government—the "on-budget" portion—back into deficit again. The social security surplus helped mask the fact (see Figure 3-3). As Sen. Daniel Moynihan (D-N.Y.) pointed out, the social security surplus provided a way to borrow from the future to pay for the present. The intended use of the social security surplus—saving for a stronger economy in the future—was being subverted to finance consumption today. Social security grew enormously in budgetary importance, became more insulated from budgetary politics, had yet produced a set of subtle accounting changes that deeply affected budgetary debate.

Medicare

Closely coupled with social security increases is the rapid rise of spending for medicare. President Johnson's "Great Society" is popularly known for its great variety of antipoverty programs. However, medicare, created in 1965 to provide medical care for the

58   *Deficit Politics*

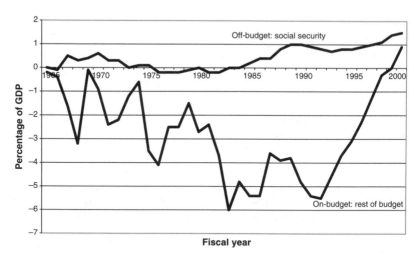

Fiscal year

Figure 3–3   On- and Off-Budget Deficits

Source: Congressional Budget Office, *The Budget and Economic Outlook: Fiscal Years 2002–2011* (Washington, D.C.: GPO, January 2001), Table 5.

elderly, proved its most important legacy. Through steady expansion of its benefits and the rising cost of medical care, Medicare is now one of the most rapidly growing federal programs. From just 3.5 percent of all federal spending in 1970, it grew to 12 percent in 2000.

Like social security, medicare is financed by a payroll tax. Unlike social security, however, medicare does not enjoy ironclad protection from budget cuts. This is because medicare operates simultaneously on three different groups of people: the elderly, who through a variety of mechanisms contribute modestly to the cost of the program; workers, who finance nearly all of it through their payroll taxes; and the medical community, which finds itself responsible, through a complex set of regulations, to the federal government for the cost and quality of care. Budgeters discovered yet again, through the 1990 budget exercise, that asking the elderly to shoulder more costs or accept fewer benefits is political suicide. The real crunch in medicare financing thus comes for the other two groups, workers and the medical establishment.

The federal government has increasingly regulated the medical establishment in an effort to restrain the hyperinflation of medical costs. Through most of the 1980s, cost increases for medical care were twice those in the rest of the economy, and as the nation's leading buyer of health services the federal government paid a large share of that increase. The federal government responded in part by ruling that some expensive or experimental procedures could not be funded through medicare. It also established in 1983 a new system of reimbursing hospitals for their costs. Known as diagnosis-related groups (DRGs), the system establishes a fixed fee for each medical problem. If an elderly patient is admitted for, say, a heart attack or a broken hip, the hospital knows in advance that the DRG system will reimburse it for only the predetermined amount. This creates great incentives in the hospitals for treating patients as quickly and inexpensively as possible; the government attempts to oversee how those services are provided to ensure that the quality of care does not suffer. The DRG system and other reforms have unquestionably slowed the spiral, but they have not restrained the overall growth rate for medicare spending.[5] The large number of elderly persons eligible for the program, their greater life expectancy thanks in part to the care provided under the program, and the rapid growth of expensive new technology all combine to push medicare expenses upward.

The continued growth of costs is just one issue the medicare program raises. Under the surface is a potentially insidious problem of equity between generations—today's retirees and today's workers. The growth of entitlement spending hides a massive shift in who benefits from federal programs. In fiscal year 1965, just 15.9 percent of the federal budget went to the elderly. By fiscal 1985, the share had nearly doubled, to 27.3 percent of all spending and 45.8 percent of domestic spending. (Throughout the period, the elderly have made up about 12 percent of the American population.) From just fiscal 1978 to 1987, federal spending for programs benefiting the elderly *increased* 52 percent, even after allowing for inflation. During the same period, federal spending for programs benefiting children *decreased* 4 percent. Families with children under 18 accounted for more than half the increase in poverty over the period, while the number of elderly families in poverty actually shrank.[6] Meanwhile, nearly all elderly Americans are covered by medicare, and most have some supplemental policy to fill in medicare gaps. Approximately 30 to 40 million nonelderly Americans of working age—more than the total number of elderly persons—are uncovered by any medical insurance plan.[7]

Such facts might well fuel a battle between young and old, as entitlement spending and especially medicare spending continues to spiral upward. Moreover, the number of middle-aged Americans, in their peak wage-earning (and tax-paying) years is increasing rapidly while the number of senior citizens is remaining about the same. This shift in population, the growth of entitlement spending, and the emerging limits on government's largesse could well shape harsh conflicts to come. By the middle of the twenty-first century, some analysts suggest, spending on the elderly will account for 40 percent of the entire gross national product.[8]

Effects on the Budget Debate

One can debate endlessly whether more federal dollars ought to be spent on the elderly or on children. It is not debatable, however, that spending for the elderly enjoys a privileged and protected place in budgetary politics—and that the questions on spending more on children and less on the elderly, for example, are therefore never asked. As Senator Bob Dole (R-Kans.) put it, "Somebody mentions the word 'medicare,' it is like crying 'fire' in a crowded theater."[9] Furthermore, the elderly's privileged place in the budget debate is based on a political claim of "entitlement," and not necessarily need. Medicare and social security, in particular, have dramatically cut the rate of poverty for the elderly. In the meantime, the group of the population at greatest risk of poverty has come to be children. Former chairman of the president's Council of Economic Advisers Herbert Stein argues that these budgetary patterns produce real problems for society. "Too much of the national output is consumed by or for people who are not poor, including what is spent for their medical care. As a corollary, too little is devoted to investment, including education, and to provision for the poor. The key requirement of a good budget policy is that it should help correct this misallocation of the national output."[10]

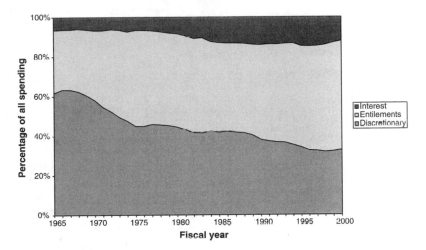

Figure 3–4   Controllable Spending

Source: Congressional Budget Office, *The Budget and Economic Outlook: Fiscal Years 2002–2011* (Washington, D.C.: GPO, January 2001), Table 9.

Budgeting is a fundamentally political process, and the key decisions shaping the budget are made by political imperatives, not by assessing who is most in need. Most entitlements go to the elderly on the basis of implied "contracts" between them and the government. Entitlement spending is the main force driving federal spending upward, but the political forces behind entitlements make restraining their growth extremely difficult. If budget makers seek to cut domestic spending, they are left with trying to cut discretionary programs. In the early 1980s, however, all of the easy cuts in discretionary programs had been made. Those cuts left that part of the budget smaller and full of programs such as air-traffic control, the FBI, AIDS research, care of the environment, and other programs that we could not cut without jeopardizing safety or cutting more deeply than most citizens are willing to accept. The decade of budget cutting during the 1980s left relatively little "fat" that budget makers could eliminated (Figure 3–4).

In debating domestic policy, it is increasingly hard to find discretionary programs to cut, and it increasingly difficult to build political support for reducing entitlement spending. Policy makers thus have less and less control over more and more of the budget.

Programs under Stress

As less of the budget became controllable, the rising share of the budget dominated by entitlements presented policy makers with tough economic and political problems. Especially in social security and medicare, elected officials faced large numbers of politically active beneficiaries who expected their benefits. Indeed, the political rhetoric surrounding social security, in particular, had long led beneficiaries to believe that they were simply getting back what they had put into the program. When proposals to trim medicare surfaced in the 1996 presidential campaign, worried seniors told candidates, "Keep the government's hands off my medicare!" They had no sense that it *was* a government program from which they received far more than they had ever paid in.

In social security and medicare, public officials had created programs that proved enormously popular with their recipients—and where benefits were guaranteed. However, by the early 1980s, it was becoming increasingly clear that in the long run the program would not be able to sustain itself. In fact, the Congressional Budget Office projected in 2001 that, by 2016, the program would begin paying out more than it was taking in. By 2040, according to some estimates, the program would be broke—it would have no more reserves from which to pay benefits (see Figure 3–5). The programs' financial problems stem from two interrelated trends: shifting demographics and indexing of benefits.

DEMOGRAPHICS.   Three trends came together at the beginning of the twenty-first century.[11] First, the baby boomers—born between 1946 and 1964—were nearing retirement. The birth rate had been far lower in earlier years, but after World War II the population surged, resulting in many more recipients entitled to benefits for senior citizens.

Second, people are living longer. When social security first began paying monthly benefits in 1940, an average 65-year-old man lived another 12.7 years. The average woman lived a bit longer, 14.7 years,

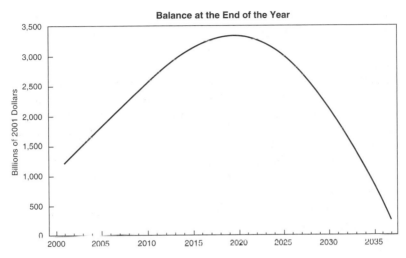

Figure 3-5   Financial Trend in Social Security

Source: Social Security Administration, *The 2001 Annual Report of the Board of Trustees of the Federal Old-Age and Survivors Insurance and Disability Insurance Trust Funds* (March 19, 2001), Table VI.E8 (intermediate assumptions).

almost to 80. In 2001, experts estimated that the average 65-year-old man would live another 16.3 years and the average woman would live another 19.6 years, almost to age 85. Moreover, analysts expected that continued improvements in health care would allow people to live even longer in the coming decades. That further increases the number of beneficiaries.

Finally, the number of workers available to support the baby boomers' retirement costs is expected to grow at a slower rate. Experts expect that the labor force will grow only slightly, just as the number of retirees grows rapidly. That means there will be fewer workers to support each retiree—and that the burden on each worker will grow. In the last half of the twentieth century, benefits for social security and medicare grew rapidly but, because of the size of the baby boomer population, the workforce grew rapidly too. As the situation switches, with more retirees and fewer workers, the programs' long-term financial situation has become more precarious.

INDEXING. Worsening the flow of red ink in the social security program was the indexation of the program's benefits. Before 1972, social security benefits were increased only through changes in the law. Congress and the president increased benefits periodically, usually around election time. In 1972, for example, Congress and President Nixon agreed on a benefit increase, which took effect in October just weeks before the presidential election. Lest anyone forget which president signed the benefits increase, a special insert accompanying the October social security check, conspicuously showing President Nixon's name, announced the increase. At the same time, the president and Congress decided to index social security payments to the cost of living. That, they reasoned, would prevent election-year shenanigans and ensure that the elderly did not suffer from inflation. The costs of indexation at the time did not seem onerous, but decision makers picked precisely the wrong time, from the budgetary point of view, to begin indexation. Shortly after the increase was passed, inflation quickly began mounting, which drove social security payments ever upward. As payments escalated, the number of recipients increased, and the number and productivity of workers supporting the program declined, social security deficits soared.

The decision to index social security payments thus set the stage for huge, automatic boosts in spending. It also laid the foundation for a spread of indexation to many other governmental programs. By 1980, ninety different programs, amounting to about half of all federal spending, carried automatic spending increases tied to the rate of inflation.[12] Federal spending became much more uncontrollable, while persistent inflation steadily drove spending upward. Indexation, in social security and other federal programs, accounted for a substantial share of the increase in entitlement spending.

These two forces shape a collision: more workers—entitled to higher benefits, with the benefits indexed and driven upward automatically—and fewer workers (and, therefore, taxpayers) to support them. Experts have differed widely on just how large a problem this is, with analyses differing from "major crisis" to "serious problem." No one thinks that it is a problem that can be ignored—or one that can fix itself.

Reforms

As the programs' problems became better known, public officials came forward with a host of reform options. Conservatives, eager to control government spending, reined in entitlements, promoted private investment, and proposed sweeping fixes that would allow individuals to create private individual investment accounts. Liberals, concerned about protecting the legacy of social security and medicare, argued for smaller changes that would shore up the programs' finances and allow continuing benefits. Among the major options are:

- *Increasing taxes.* The fundamental problem, according to analysts, is that the likely cost of the programs' benefits will exceed available resources by the middle of the twenty-first century. One possibility is to increase taxes on workers at that point to pay the benefits. With fewer workers to support each beneficiary, however, the extra taxes would be substantial and would choke economic growth.
- *Change benefits.* Another obvious option is to reduce the amount that the programs pay out, by reducing automatic annual indexing rate, by increasing the retirement age, or both. Traditional supporters of the programs have fought these provisions furiously and have argued that they would undermine the ability of seniors to live secure, dignified lives. Moreover, as medical costs increase, medicare is accounting for a larger share of entitlement spending, and these proposals would do little to solve that problem. Indeed, proposals to expand medicare by providing prescription drug coverage to seniors would make the long-term financial problem even worse.
- *Create and save a federal budget surplus.* Some reformers propose that the federal government ought to shift its taxing and spending policies now to produce larger budget surpluses. Those surpluses could be used to pay off the national debt, which would increase the government's ability to afford the larger entitlement payments. Continued surpluses could then be invested in private-sector stocks and bonds, which would be

cashed in when needed to pay for the baby boomers' retirement costs. However, some observers have wondered how the government could manage a private investment portfolio: What investments would be appropriate—and what would not? If the federal government becomes a shareholder, how could it exercise its ownership responsibilities without interfering in the private market?

- *Transfer some—or all—of social security into private retirement accounts.* Conservative analysts have long pointed out that social security has a relatively low rate of return for investors. Much of that, however, occurs because early generations of retirees received far more benefits back than they had paid in. The more social security relies on private investments by individuals, the less the program can play its current role of building a floor under the monthly payments that retirees receive—especially for those who did not have high-paying jobs or who receive payments because of their spouse's careers. Moreover, the more the program relies on private investment, the riskier is the return. Private investments pay higher rates of return than social security because they carry much greater risks. Most employees at energy trading giant Enron saw their private retirement accounts completely wiped out in 2001 when the company went broke. Even ordinary investors suffered a serious decline when total stock market returns in 2001 dropped more than 11 percent.

As the programs' long-term situation weakened, policy makers scrambled to find an option that would strengthen the finances without incurring the political wrath of beneficiaries—current and future. Democrats tried to portray Republicans as reckless and insensitive; Republicans tried to picture Democrats as irresponsible free-spenders. Conservatives tried to disassemble portions of the public entitlements and transfer more wealth to the private sector; liberals struggled to maintain the programs' historic base. It was little wonder, therefore, that social security and medicare had become the toughest political and economic problems facing federal budget makers.

Tax Policy

Since the late 1970s, antitax sentiment has periodically swelled in American politics. California voters approved Proposition 13 in 1978 to restrain the growth of local property taxes. Ronald Reagan picked up on that theme in the 1980 presidential campaign, by promising to balance the budget by lowering taxes. The promise was not quite so outlandish as it seemed at first. The federal personal income tax rates were too high, he said. Lowering them might cost some revenue at first but would encourage everyone to earn more money, since they would be able to keep more of it. Corporate income taxes were even worse, in his opinion, because they created incentives against high corporate profits. Cutting tax rates, Reagan reasoned, would therefore increase revenues. This strategy was known as "supply-side" economics, because it was devoted to increasing incentives to supply goods and services rather than increasing their demand through higher government spending. Congress approved Reagan's supply-side approach in 1981 by cutting personal income tax rates by nearly one fourth. The corporate income tax was virtually eliminated through special preferences written into the tax code.

President Reagan trumpeted his 1981 victory as the largest tax cut in American history. It was followed in 1982, however, by major tax increases and in 1983 by one of the biggest tax increases in history, the hike in payroll taxes to put the social security program back on its feet. In fact, there were tax increases in every year of the Reagan administration but 1981 and 1986. President Reagan remained best known for the tax cuts, and George Bush rode the theme to election in 1988 with his famous "Read my lips—no new taxes!" promise.

When George W. Bush won election in 2000, he picked up the tax cut banner. He made a major Reagan-style tax cut the first item on his agenda. In fact, he argued for cutting taxes even before Congress passed the budget or determined how much the government's programs would cost. As with the Reagan tax cut, the plan was in part to use tax cuts to restrain future spending growth. Cutting taxes would take money out of the government's hands and reduce the temptation to spend it in future years. At the time, huge surpluses loomed over the next decade, and Bush wanted to put a brake on the impulse to increase government programs. When the big surpluses turned into deficits a year later, the Democrats tried to blame Bush for plunging the budget back into crisis again.

Since even before the Boston Tea Party, Americans have resented taxes. Few businesses are more imaginative or more lucrative than the industry of finding legal ways around paying taxes. Individuals sometimes buy large houses for the tax breaks (since the interest cost of the mortgage as well as local property taxes on the house are deductible expenses). Corporations sometimes snap up other corporations purely for tax advantage. Individual businesspeople sometimes prefer accepting cash for payment because that makes it harder for the Internal Revenue Service to track their income, and the IRS has spent years trying to capture income taxes on the tips earned by servers in restaurants. If the budget needs to be brought closer into balance, most Americans would prefer to see the government's spending brought down to the level of revenues instead of raising taxes to the level of expenditures.

It is little secret, therefore, that Americans think their taxes are too high, and it is a fair guess that most Americans think their federal taxes have risen over the years. However, when measured as a share of the gross national product (GNP), federal taxes have been steady at about 18 or 19 percent of the GNP since the late 1960s. In fact, except for a brief dip in the mid-1950s, when the economy was growing and government tax policy remained relatively stable, federal receipts have remained about 18 or 19 percent of the GNP since the Korean War.

This surprising fact raises an important question. Tax cuts, from President Kennedy's 1963 cut and President Reagan's 1981 cut, have been regular features of budgetary politics. How could taxes be cut but the overall level of revenues stay the same? The reason lies in the composition of federal revenues, as Figure 3–6 shows.

Income Taxes

The irony is that, despite frequent income tax cuts, the income tax burden since the Korean War in the 1950s has been remarkably level as a share of the economy. In fact, individual income taxes have

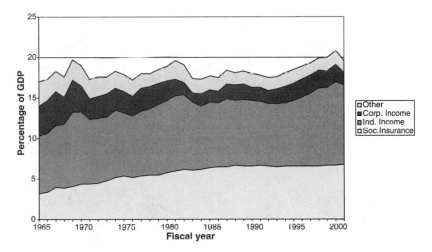

Figure 3-6 Federal Government Revenues

Source: Congressional Budget Office, *The Budget and Economic Outlook: Fiscal Years 2002–2011* (Washington, D.C.: GPO, January 2001), Table 7.

accounted for between 45 and 50 percent of federal receipts since 1950. Despite the regular cuts, the income tax burden has stayed about the same.

How can the burden have stayed level despite income tax cuts? Economic growth and inflation together have steadily pushed individuals' incomes up. Higher incomes have brought greater revenues. Moreover, especially before 1981, higher levels of income pushed income taxes up. This escalation of taxes was a product of two features of the tax code: tax brackets and the marginal rate. A *tax bracket* is a range of income (say, from $25,000 to $50,000) to which a tax rate applies. As income rises, individuals move to higher tax brackets. Along with that move comes a higher *marginal rate*, the rate the individual pays on the last dollars he or she earns. The first dollars of income are tax free, the next level of income is taxed at low income tax rates, and the highest level of income is taxed at higher income tax rates. As individuals move into higher tax brackets, they pay higher marginal rates. (For an example of how the tax brackets and the marginal rates have changed over the years, see Table 3–1.)

Deficit Politics

Table 3-1   Changes in Tax Policy

	Bottom Bracket		Top Bracket	
Year	Rate (percent)	On Taxable Income up to (dollars)	Rate (percent)	On Taxable Income over (dollars)
1913	1	20,000	7	500,000
1920	4	4,000	73	1,000,000
1930	1.12	4,000	25	100,000
1940	4.4	4,000	81.1	5,000,000
1950	17.4	4,000	91	400,000
1960	20	4,000	91	400,000
1970	14	1,000	71.75	200,000
1980	14	2,100	70	212,000
1991	15	34,000	31	82,150
2001	15	27,050	39.1	297,350

Note: The federal personal income tax was introduced in 1913.

Source: Committee on Ways and Means, House of Representatives, *Overview of the Federal Tax System*, 101st Cong., 2d sess., 1990, pp. 44–45; news reports; and information from the Internal Revenue Service and the White House.

This system has several important effects. The *average* tax rate an individual pays is usually less than the *marginal* rate, since the first dollars are untaxed and lower levels of income are taxed at lower rates. If marginal rates are high in the upper brackets, furthermore, the amount of each extra dollar of income that an individual gets to keep shrinks the higher the income goes. This argument was at the core of Reagan's supply-side revolution. Higher-income individuals have little incentive to earn more income if they keep little of the extra money they earn. A key incentive is that such individuals generate much of the nation's economic growth, through consumption, investment, and entrepreneurial activity. The stronger incentive they have to work hard and make more money, the better off everyone else will be. Thus, both the 1981 and 1986 tax reforms had at their core the collapse of tax brackets into a much smaller number and a much lower top marginal rate.

The overall result of these changes is that the much-publicized reductions in individual income taxes have, over the years, almost precisely matched the long-run tendency of income tax receipts to rise as individuals make more money. The cuts have periodically returned to individuals' pockets the money that inflation and increases in productivity have taken away. This, however, creates yet another puzzle: If individual income tax receipts have stayed remarkably level, why do individuals think that their taxes have gone up?

Payroll Taxes

The taxes paid by individuals in fact have risen substantially since the 1960s. The reason is that the payroll tax paid to support social security and medicare has increased very rapidly. In 1960, the payroll tax amounted to just less than 3 percent of the GDP. By 2001, it was more than twice as high, at 7 percent. Over the same period, the payroll tax grew from 16 to 35 percent of all federal government receipts (see Figure 3–6).

These taxes are much more hidden than are income taxes. To be sure, in each paycheck every wage earner sees the money disappearing in the "FICA" column. Taxpayers, however, do not have to total the payroll tax at the end of the year to see how much they have paid, as they must when filing the federal income tax form. Their employers contribute an equal amount on their behalf, and they never see that amount. Economists assume that the burden of the employers' share is borne in the end by employees, in the form of wages that are lower than would otherwise be the case. The income tax provides individuals with exemptions and deductions so that individuals have to make a substantial amount of money—$18,250 for a family of four in 2002—before having to pay any income tax. The burden of the payroll tax has gradually been creeping upward, but in a way that disguises its costs.

Other Taxes

Putting the two major taxes paid by individuals together—the personal income tax and the payroll tax—reveals a major shift over time in the tax burden. From 1960 to 2001, the share of all federal receipts accounted for by these two taxes grew from 60 to 85 percent. Other taxes shrank in importance at the same time. The income tax on corporate profits, which accounted for one fourth of all federal receipts in the mid-1950s, fell to just 8 percent in 2001. Other federal receipts—from the excise tax on gasoline and tires to estate taxes and customs duties—have dropped from 16 to 7 percent of all receipts. Each new deficit battle produces new ways of raising some of these "all other" taxes, such as increasing gasoline and liquor taxes. Compared to the total amount of revenue the federal government raises, and contrasted with the huge increases over the years in payroll taxes for social security and medicare, these tax hikes are trivial. The central features of American tax policy since World War II are the relatively steady share of individual income taxes, despite several major tax cuts; the enormous growth of payroll taxes; and the declining share of all other forms of revenue.

The subtle shift in tax policy has had important implications for who bears the federal tax burden. Because of the rapid increase in social insurance payroll taxes, many middle-class families pay more in payroll taxes than in federal income taxes. The more the federal tax burden shifts to payroll taxes, the greater the burden will be on lower-income individuals. As we have seen, payroll taxes are imposed from the first dollar earned and stop above a certain income level. The result is a wide spread in the effective tax rate for individuals, as a Congressional Budget Office study has found (see Figure 3–7).

Tax policy has for decades been squeezed between competing, and often conflicting, objectives. Budget makers have sought to increase the incentives for investment, and hence for economic growth, by reducing individual income tax rates and by significantly reducing the corporate income tax. They have struggled to finance the social security and medicare programs by increasing the payroll tax. They have tried to reduce the burden on the poor by lowering the individual income tax's demand on the poor. Above all, they have labored to reduce the budget deficit.

The net result of these battles is that the government's overall tax burden, measured by the share of the GNP it takes through taxes, has stayed almost exactly the same. Along the way, the tax mix has changed, with far more reliance on the payroll tax. For the poorest members of society, changes in the individual income tax and in

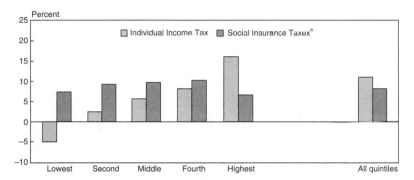

Figure 3–7   Effective Federal Tax Rates, 1997

Source: Congressional Budget Office.
Notes: The effective tax rate equals tax liabilities as a percentage of total income.
Quintiles, or fifths, of the income distribution contain equal numbers of people.
[a] Payroll taxes financing social security, medicare, and federal unemployment insurance.

federal benefit programs have about canceled out the payroll tax increases. For the middle of American society, however, the overall tax burden, especially for payroll taxes, has increased. And it is from the middle class that the strongest complaints about the tax burden have come.

These interlocking trends have important implications for reducing the deficit. Despite the annual, frantic search for new revenue sources that do not look like taxes, the federal government has continued to rely more on taxes, principally payroll taxes, on individuals. The burden for paying these taxes is falling more heavily on the middle class. Budget makers, meanwhile, have had little real flexibility in raising other taxes.

Tax Preferences

One place where there is a great deal of money is in special tax preferences granted through the tax code. Some of these tax breaks are *deductions*, which allow taxpayers (individual and corporate) to subtract certain expenditures from their income before paying taxes.

Some are *exemptions*, which allow taxpayers to avoid paying tax on some kinds of income (such as interest on borrowing by state and local governments). Finally, some are *credits*, which allow taxpayers to reduce their tax bill by the amount of an expenditure. Most of the complexity of the income tax system, in fact, comes from trying to navigate through the vast array of special tax provisions. Without them, the income tax return could easily fit on a postcard. With them, many Americans rely on complex computer programs to help them fill out their taxes, or they hire private companies like H&R Block to do the job for them.

Some preferences are special deductions that corporations can use in depreciating (or writing off the expense of) equipment. Others allow individuals to deduct the cost of mortgage interest and property taxes on their homes and to exempt the value of health insurance purchased by employers from their income. (See Table 3–2 for examples of tax preferences.) As with entitlements, there is no appropriation for the programs. The total of tax preferences is determine by who is eligible for them and how they use them. The programs have a huge impact; were they eliminated, hundreds of billions of dollars would annually flow back into the federal treasury.

As attractive as this grab bag of possible revenue sources might be, eliminating the hundreds of special tax breaks would require untold political strength. Each tax preference has a special group of defenders for whom it is critical, and who are willing to spend large amounts of money to protect it. Some preferences, such as the home mortgage deduction, are simply politically untouchable. Tax reforms, especially the 1986 act, have significantly improved the tax code's fairness. There nevertheless remain huge sources of potential revenue, sources that are often impregnable to attack because of the power of the political forces defending them.

Shrinking Discretion

The ultimate issue of deficit politics is this: As the budget and its deficit have become larger issues, both politically and economically, the options open to decision makers to control the budget have shrunk. Federal expenditures, no matter how measured, have

Table 3-2 Top Ten Tax Preferences

	Revenue Effects, Fiscal Year 2003 (millions of dollars)
1. Exclusion of employer contributions for medical insurance premiums and medical care	99,260
2. Deductibility of mortgage interest on owner-occupied homes	66,110
3. Capital gains	60,200
4. Net exclusion of pension contributions and earnings: 401(k) plans	59,510
5. Net exclusion of pension contributions and earnings: Employer plans	53,080
6. Deductibility of nonbusiness state and local taxes other than on owner occupied homes	48,150
7. Accelerated depreciation of machinery and equipment	36,480
8. Deductibility of charitable contributions, other than education and health	32,080
9. Step-up basis of capital gains at death	28,710
10. Exclusion of interest on public purpose state and local bonds	24,720

Source: Office of Management and Budget, *Budget of the United States Government, Fiscal Year 2003: Analytical Perspectives* (Washington, D.C.: Government Printing Office, 2002).

increased substantially since World War II and, especially, since the early 1970s. Calls to reduce federal spending are heard regularly, but the major force driving spending upward is the nation's collection of entitlement programs. Social security and medicare dominate entitlements, and these programs are politically formidable. America's new role in the world is forcing a reevaluation of defense spending. The overall structure of the federal budget, however, makes significant changes extremely difficult. Eliminating the deficit through budget cuts alone is virtually impossible.

No one wants to raise taxes and the very structure of the revenue side reduces the options. Federal receipts are dominated by individual income and payroll taxes. The Democrats have lost two presidential campaigns, in part, for even suggesting income tax increases. Opposition to higher payroll taxes continues to be strong, both among those who must pay them and among those who contend that raising them would make the tax system far less fair.

This is not to say that budget makers have no options. They do not, however, have any attractive options. Social security and medicare can be cut or transformed, and the defense budget can be further trimmed. Tax preferences can be scaled back or eliminated. Income tax rates can be increased. Any of these would be hard to do, but history suggests that only a combination of several initiatives is likely to produce genuine deficit reduction and budget stability. For elected officials who have to defend such decisions, it is bad enough to attack any one of these sacred cows. It is far, far worse to have to assault more than one at a time.

Given the simple arithmetic of the budget's basic choices, it is little wonder that it is so contentious. Deficit politics is a natural product of the decisions that the structure of the budget presents. Furthermore, given how hard it is to find good answers to these problems, it is little wonder that the process has so often become deadlocked and broken down. Budget makers have long sought some better way to make these tough choices, and we turn next to the enduring search for rationality in the budgetary process.

Notes

1. "Budget Message of the President," February 4, 2002.
2. *Wall Street Journal*, February 7, 1991, p. A16.
3. *New York Times*, February 3, 1991, Sec. 1, p. 14; and February 5, 1991, p. A13.
4. Ibid., p. 288.
5. See Peter G. Peterson and Neil Howe, *On Borrowed Time: How the Growth in Entitlement Spending Threatens America's Futures* (San Francisco: ICS Press), chap. 5.

6. House of Representatives, Committee on Ways and Means, *Background Material and Data on Programs Within the Jurisdiction of the Committee on Ways and Means: Overview of Entitlement Programs* (1990 Green Book), 101st Cong., 2d sess., 1990, pp. 1055, 1061–6.
7. Howe and Peterson, *On Borrowed Time*, p. 202.
8. *National Journal* 23 (February 23, 1991), p. 478.
9. *New York Times*, October 19, 1990, p. A10.
10. Herbert Stein, "The 1990 Budget Package," *The American Enterprise* 2 (January/February 1991), p. 8.
11. Congressional Budget Office, *Social Security: A Primer* (GPO, September 2001), pp. 29–32.
12. R. Kent Weaver, *Automatic Government: The Politics of Indexation* (Washington, D.C.: Brookings Institution, 1988), p. 1. Approximately 30 percent of the federal budget is directly tied to the consumer price index, while another 20 percent is indirectly indexed.

CHAPTER 4

The Search for Rationality

With so much rancor surrounding budgetary politics, it is little wonder that budget reformers have sought some way of increasing rationality in the system. The search for a rational approach to budgeting, in fact, has come to resemble the quest for the Holy Grail. Brave knights of yore believed that drinking from the grail would produce a divine vision that revealed all truth. Budget reformers likewise have searched for a magical cup whose elixir would reveal the best way to budget public money and avoid political conflict. Bureaucrats always believe they can budget more rationally. Most presidents have felt the same frustration and have struggled to impose rationality on the conflict-filled politics of federal budgeting. Even members of Congress, whom many critics hold as the villains in the story, have struggled to develop new approaches to solving the old problems.

Theoreticians, meanwhile, have long struggled to develop some way to develop clear, systematic plans for how best to spend the nation's resources.[1] At the bottom of these enduring conflicts and problems is a key question: Isn't there some better way to budget? Isn't there a way to substitute orderly thinking and formal decision rules for the rough-and-tumble politics of budgeting? Isn't there a way to "just say no" to demands that exceed available resources? Isn't there some way to decrease expectations or increase resources so promises can be kept? Isn't there a Holy Grail somewhere that can replace conflict with truth and vision?

79

Rational Analysis and Budgetary Reform

Little consolation comes from learning that the question is ageless. Political scientist V. O. Key perhaps put the problem best in 1940: "On what basis shall it be decided to allocate *x* dollars to activity A instead of activity B?"[2] In the two-hundred-year history of the United States, and in the fifty years since V. O. Key stated the puzzle, the question remains unanswered. This disappointment is not for lack of trying. There have been endless crusades, fought by brave knights with sharp lances. Yet no crusade has ever satisfied its supporters' fond hopes.

Line-Item Budgeting

Most budget reforms aim at replacing the dominant form of budgeting, *line-item budgeting*. This technique classifies financial information first by major organizational units, such as the Department of Agriculture, and then by subunits, such as Office of the Secretary, the Farmers Home Administration, and the Soil Conservation Service. Within these subcategories, spending then is usually broken down by accounts. The Farmers Home Administration, for example, provides housing assistance for rural areas. Accounts within its budget include salaries, rural water grants, rural fire protection grants, rural housing for farm labor, rural housing repair grants, and rural development grants. The Environmental Protection Agency (EPA) has accounts for salaries, research and development, pollution abatement and control, construction grants, a "superfund" to help clean up hazardous wastes, and another fund to cure the problem of leaking underground storage tanks.

Line-item budgeting provides a great deal of information about *who* in government does *what*. It literally lists, on different lines, the items on which the government spends its money. The problem with this approach, however, is that it tells very little about *how well* the money is being spent. If EPA spends $1.5 billion on the superfund program, is the nation's massive hazardous waste program any closer to solution? Spending money does not guarantee results. What budget makers want to know is what results government programs achieve, not how much they spend. Put differently, if they face tough choices about putting more money into program A or program B, which program will produce better results? This, of course, is a reformulation of Key's famous question. Line-item budgeting cannot provide the answer, and that has set the stage for endless budget reforms: reforms to provide a clear link between the budget's inputs—the dollars spent—and its outputs—the benefits received. Armed with such knowledge, reformers have long hoped, they could improve the rationality with which budgetary decisions are made.

The Incrementalist Response

Some scholars, however, have long challenged the idea that a rational approach to budgeting is either possible or desirable. Foremost among these critics is Charles E. Lindblom, whose classic article, "The Science of Muddling Through," argued that it is paradoxically more rational to avoid rational analysis and that it is less rational to attempt comprehensive analysis.[3] The attempt to be a rational analyst, Lindblom contended, is doomed because:

- *No analyst can ever be comprehensive.* Complete rationality requires that analysts consider *every* option. That, of course, is impossible. Things will be left out, but the rational-comprehensive approach does not tell the analyst what to leave out. Yet without a clear answer to this problem, the analyst can never know if an important, rational alternative has been neglected.
- *Trying to do analysis requires the analyst to make impossible assumptions.* The process of simplifying the problem enough to make analysis possible requires the analyst to decide what goals to concentrate on and which alternatives are the most reasonable. No analyst can ever know which goals and alternatives are the most reasonable, Lindblom argues.

Lindblom contends instead that "successive limited comparisons"— choice among a small range of alternatives to serve limited goals— is far superior to rational-comprehensive analysis. In the end, he argues, the political process does a far better job of solving these problems than rational analysis ever can. Decision making is about value choice, and the choice of values is the central problem of politics. Thus, the argument suggests, trying to replace politics with rationality is doomed—and wrong.

Aaron Wildavsky advanced this argument in his classic, *The Politics of the Budgetary Process.*[4] Wildavsky argues that budgeting *is* and *should be* characterized by *incrementalism*, that is, by "fair-share" increases to an existing "base." Budget makers simplify their complex task by assuming, in the absence of overwhelming political pressure, continued funding for each program at existing levels, or the base. Program advocates seek to expand their programs by an amount that other participants will recognize as fair. Commonly this means that everyone gets about the same percentage increase, although a program with especially strong political support or unusual problems might get a larger increase. These increases then become folded into next year's base, and the process begins again.

Wildavsky claims that incrementalism explains how budgeting actually works. He also claims it is the superior technique for reaching budgetary decisions. It simplifies the decisions to manageable size by focusing only on changes to existing programs, instead of looking at everything from scratch. It also allocates money on the basis of a program's political strength. That, he contends, is as close as we can come to knowing which programs are most deserving.

Incrementalism has come under fierce attack from many fronts. Analysts of all stripes argue that previous decisions may be far less worthy than new ideas. Furthermore, they contend, what constitutes a "fair share" increment is determined more by a program's political support than by its intrinsic worth. Incrementalism thus strikes many critics as an apology for inefficient decision making in the budgetary process, as an enshrinement of sometimes ugly partisan squabbling, and as a roadblock to more reasonable, rational decision making. Critics also point out that incrementalism works only when the budget's size is increasing. As deficits increase, many programs can increase only at the expense of cuts in other programs. Despite these problems, incrementalism maintains a powerful hold on budgeting. It continues to condition the way many people think about budgetary decisions. To the dismay of many reformers, it helps defend existing programs from cuts and frustrates reallocation of scarce federal funds.

The debate between advocates of rational decision making and promoters of incrementalism have shaped both the study of budgeting and attempts to reform it since World War II. Five major strategies have emerged in the effort to improve rationality in budgeting:

1. Performance budgeting, in which budgeters link inputs with outputs.
2. The programming-planning-budgeting-system (PPBS), in which budgeters link program goals with program costs.
3. Management by objectives (MBO), similar to performance budgeting, in which budgeters attempted to link superiors and subordinates in a contractlike relationship to promote program performance.
4. Zero-based budgeting (ZBB), in which budgeters must make an analytical case for increases above a given base.
5. The Government Performance and Results Act (GPRA), which seeks to link strategic planning and an analysis of results directly with budget decisions.

Performance Budgeting

In 1913, the federal government's Taft Commission on Economy and Efficiency argued that government officials needed to tie public expenditures to the outcomes they produce.[5] Little was done about the suggestion until 1934, when the Department of Agriculture adopted "performance budgeting." The Tennessee Valley Authority followed suit soon afterwards, and the Hoover Commission (1949) enthusiastically recommended that the approach be widely adopted. Although performance budgeting has sometimes meant different things in different places where it has been applied, the old Bureau of the Budget defined its core concept:

> A performance budget is one which presents the purposes and objectives for which funds are required, the costs of the programs proposed for achieving those objectives, and quantitative data measuring the accomplishment and work performed under each program.[6]

Performance budgeting generally requires seven steps:[7]

1. Top managers *identify the major products* their agencies produce.
2. Where possible, they *reorganize* their agencies according to these products.
3. Managers then *identify units of performance* (e.g., miles of highway built, number of facilities inspected).
4. Managers fully *measure the costs* of their products.
5. Managers establish *internal reporting processes* so they can keep track of the performance of their programs.
6. Congress drafts *authorizing legislation in performance terms*. Rather than appropriating money for nebulous goals, Congress provides money for specific and clearly defined purposes.
7. An *accounting system* is created to track expenditures and outcomes.

The basic approach of performance budgeting is at once simple, yet radical. Performance budgeting begins by focusing attention on what government does, not who does it. It concentrates on outputs, not inputs. How much toxic waste is cleaned up? How many new units of housing are provided? How many unemployed workers get jobs because of government job-training programs? By concentrating on outputs, decision makers can better budget, the advocates of performance budgeting argue, because they have a better idea of what they are buying.

The idea is so simple and powerful that it is easy to overlook the problems in implementing it. It is often not legally possible or politically easy to reorganize an agency according to its work products. Organizational structures develop their own constituencies, which are hard to uproot. Furthermore, developing clear outcome measures, especially about the quality instead of the volume of work, is often deceptively difficult. Input measures, such as the number of applications processed, are often easy to gauge, but it is far more difficult to judge the results they produce. In addition, many parts of the bureaucracy, particularly staff agencies such as personnel, budgeting, and auditing, do not have outputs that can be clearly identified. (Table 4–1 summarizes performance budgeting, as well as the other budget reform ideas.)

The most important contribution of performance budgeting is its focus on budgetary outputs instead of inputs. The federal government has never successfully adopted performance budgeting in its pure form, however. On one hand, some critics argue that it is far too ambitious because it requires more changes than the government or its administrators can manage. On the other hand, other critics contend that it is not ambitious enough because more sophisticated techniques could improve budgeting even further. This argument has led to new reforms, beginning with the planning-programming-budgeting system.

Planning-Programming Budgeting Systems

When Robert McNamara came to the Pentagon in 1961, he was unhappy with the competition he found among the military services. Too often, he believed, the services proposed weapons systems to enhance their own budgets instead of serving the nation's broader strategic needs. In fact, McNamara maintained that systems purchased for one service could sometimes serve another service's needs, without having to pay the huge costs for developing a new and different weapon. With the aid of bright microeconomists, dubbed his "whiz kids," McNamara introduced the Planning-Programming-Budgeting System (PPBS) to revolutionize Pentagon budgeting.[8]

The application of PPBS varied greatly throughout the government, but it generally pursued a three-step process:

1. Budgeters would first *plan their goals*, by considering alternative ways to reach their targets and choosing the best one. PPBS thus developed from a strategic plan.
2. Budgeters would then *program*. That is, they would determine what combination of manpower, facilities, materials, and other resources would be needed to accomplish the plan. The strategic plan would lead to shorter range objectives.
3. Finally, budgeters would *budget*. Programming would help them determine *which* resources were needed *when*. The goals thus drove the program, and the program drove the budget.

Table 4–1 Strategies to Reform the Federal Budgetary Process

Technique	When Introduced	Approach	Problems	Fate
Performance budgeting	Taft Commission (1913); Dept. of Agriculture (1934); Hoover Commission (1949)	Link inputs (dollars) with outputs (performance measures)	Often does not provide information about overall effectiveness; good cost accounting systems frequently not present	Superseded by PPBS but still frequently used
Planning-programming-budgeting system	In Pentagon: 1961; in rest of federal government: 1965	Budgeting by program; obtain *total* program costs	Bureaucratic inertia; analytical burdens; political subversion of system	Replaced by Nixon with MBO
Management by objectives	1973	Decentralized budgeting with management links	Apolitical emphasis on management diminished support; Watergate politics preoccupied all	Replaced by Carter with ZBB
Zero-base budgeting	1976	Rank ordering of "decision packages"	Much of federal budget uncontrollable; large paperwork burden; easily subverted	Abandoned by Reagan
Government Performance and Results Act	1993	Connect spending with results	Strategic planning, performance Measurements are difficult; use of performance information by elected officials uneven	?

For example, both the air force and the navy needed new fighter-bombers. McNamara pressed each service to define the missions that the planes would need to accomplish. These mission statements drove the design of the plane, and the design then determined the plane's budget. The plane, first dubbed the TFX and then the F-111, had problems at first, and the navy was never satisfied with its version. The air force, however, used the plane successfully in the raid launched against Libya in 1986 and in the 1991 war against Iraq.

Through PPBS, McNamara's whiz kids hoped to escape the demands of the individual services and the short-term focus of annual budgeting. They developed a five-year plan that embodied basic missions. The missions cut across organizational boundaries and grouped together similar activities, such as close air support of ground forces or airlift and sealift of troops and materials. The five-year plans were updated, so that budgeters were always looking into the future. Furthermore, all costs relating to individual systems were grouped together. Research, development, production, deployment, and maintenance costs of each system were all assigned to that system, instead of to the organizational unit doing the work, as would have been the case in traditional line-item budgeting.

PPBS was more goal-oriented than performance budgeting, because it required planners to map their broad aims before moving ahead. It had a longer horizon than previous budgeting systems, since it required budgeters to plan five years down the road. And it surmounted the organizational problems of performance budgeting. Instead of requiring organizations to be reorganized by their outputs, it allocated funds across organizational units by program. President Lyndon B. Johnson was so impressed with the changes PPBS had brought in the Pentagon that he ordered in August 1965 that all domestic agencies adopt PPB systems.

The bright hopes of PPBS were soon tarnished, however. In the civilian agencies, the planning burdens soon overwhelmed the system. Wags suggested that the entire government was sagging under the burden of file cabinets holding voluminous PPBS reports that no one, especially in the budget offices, had time to read. Meanwhile, Congress curiously was left out of the entire process. PPB-prepared budgets did not fit either Congress's structure or the way it made budgetary policy. Congress is organized by committees and subcommittees that review individual agencies. It also appropriates money not by program but by the traditional line-item form. Elaborate systems were required to translate PPBS documents back into the form that Congress needed. PPBS in concept made much sense. In operation, it proved an enormous paperwork burden—and the paper did not fit the way those who made budgetary decisions thought about the budget.

In the wake of problems in the domestic agencies and in the State Department, the Nixon administration officially abandoned PPBS. The budgeting system scarcely died, however. Five-year plans even today remain a staple of Pentagon planning and budgeting, even if they do not carry the tarnished PPBS label. PPBS, in fact, not only lives but thrives in modified form. Where it worked best, it was because agency decision makers saw benefits to their own operations; there was an ample supply of skilled analysts; and the analysts had both formal and informal access to agency decision makers.[9]

In short, PPBS performed badly when simply imposed by mandate on agencies, when agency officials viewed it as a necessary evil, when agencies had "soft" outputs (such as foreign-policy negotiations), and when it did not fit the needs of budget makers. Not surprisingly, PPBS worked very poorly in the State Department. As one departmental official complained:

> It is virtually impossible (in many or most or all) foreign affairs activities to measure outputs in terms of national objectives. Cost effectiveness analyses in these fields would be futile or even seriously misleading by directing attention only to things that might be measured and ignoring other, perhaps are more important outcomes. Some of the most important and effective decisions in foreign affairs are virtually costless in terms of dollars. Foreign affairs (all or most of it) is ultimately political in purpose; and politics can't be measured.[10]

PPBS did best when it fit the agency's culture and was viewed as a useful tool by agency officials. In the Pentagon, where officials were long used to working with long-term projects (design of a new weapons system can take years), where outputs could be identified (an antimissile system works when it knocks an incoming missile out of the sky), and where officials were used to considering such analytical issues (succeeding generations of McNamara's whiz kids still populate the Pentagon, but not in such large numbers) variations of PPBS have endured. When PPBS proved not to be the Holy Grail for which crusaders searched, new ideas surfaced. The next cup to be tried was management by objectives.

Management by Objectives

Presidents rarely have been eager to continue budget reforms introduced by their predecessors, especially when that predecessor belonged to the other party. The Nixon administration therefore introduced in 1973 its own reform, "management by objectives" (MBO). MBO was already widely used in industry and fit the administration's tactics to improve public management, including renaming the Bureau of the Budget as the Office of Management and Budget (OMB). Unlike PPBS, which was purely a budgetary program, MBO was a management technique loosely coupled with budgeting. Managers were to set clear and measurable objectives for their organizations and staff to accomplish them. These objectives would then shape budgetary decisions.[11]

MBO tended to focus more than PPBS on workload measures. MBO was also designed to improve communications among different parts of the government. Top officials would decide what they wanted the agency or department to accomplish. These objectives were then to be broken down into the pieces to be accomplished at different levels of the bureaucracy. The top officials, for example, might define one objective as reducing the time required to process grant applications by 10 percent. A subordinate might then agree to reorganize the filing system during the coming year, which would speed up the application flow. The superior would then have clear objectives by which to judge the subordinate's performance. All the objectives of individual employees, folded back together, would help the agency better achieve its broad objectives.

In the end, MBO's advocates hoped, managers would be better able to motivate their workers, since the objectives would be the product of far more consultation. They would be better able to judge their agency's success, since they would know what individuals had agreed to accomplish. Finally, they would be able to budget better, since the connections among people, programs, outcomes, and money would be better defined.

MBO broke down in implementation, however.[12] Its problems stemmed not so much from differences among agencies' output as variances in the way MBO was applied at different levels of government. To avoid the much-criticized constraints of PPBS, OMB set only fuzzy policy for how MBO ought to be done. The objectives set by agencies therefore varied enormously. Moreover, the natural tendencies of administrators at different levels tended to produce relatively useless and noncontroversial objectives:

1. *Most objectives had little broad meaning.* Most MBO objectives dealt with "inside-the-Beltway" activities that carried little weight outside Washington.

2. *MBO became turned upside down.* Although OMB intended to be generated from the top down, it became dominated by objectives defined from the bottom up. Top officials tended to get only catalogues of objectives produced by lower-level officials and passed up with little modification. Low-level officials tended to see agency problems myopically, and higher-level officials did little to pull broader policy from the objectives.

3. *Managers learned to define easy-to-accomplish objectives.* The objectives tended to be relatively uncontroversial. Higher-level administrators were careful about defining objectives that could create political trouble. Lower-level officials rarely set objectives that were not already nearly met. Such defensive action produced objectives that gave top officials little leverage on the process.

Whatever MBO might have contributed to federal management and budgeting, the Watergate scandal drove out attention to all but the immediate problems of keeping the government moving. Nearly everyone, especially members of Congress, became suspicious of the reforms that the Nixon administration had introduced. Changes touted as "management improvements" were especially suspect because the administration's opponents feared that the "improvements" would prove a ruse for cutting programs or for increasing the president's power.

MBO disappointed its most ardent fans. Like PPBS, however, it did not disappear. Indeed, as political scientist Richard Rose has argued, it "evaporated," leaving a residue of interest in management issues behind.[13] It tended to work best, and to last longest, in agencies where communication among levels of the organization was the norm. It also tended to work best in agencies where objectives were easily counted, such as bureaus that processed applications or paved roads. It tended to fail where it asked managers to behave in a way that threatened the existing culture and to quantify activities, such as planning, research, and development, that did not easily lend themselves to measurement. With the end of the Nixon administration, moreover, interest in budgeting-as-management largely disappeared as well.

Zero-Base Budgeting

Jimmy Carter came into office having run against Washington, determined to shake up the bureaucracy. When he came to town he brought with him the zero-base budgeting (ZBB) system he had developed in Georgia. ZBB had, at its core, the idea of never assuming that agencies were entitled to continued funding for their programs simply because they had received funds the year before. In theory, budgeting would begin from a "zero base," and any increases over past funding would have to be won in an analytical competition with other proposals. ZBB thus was an implicit attack on incrementalism, which assumed that funding would continue at least at the level of the previous year's budget (the base) and that increases would be determined by bargaining. Versions of the system had been used as far back as 1924, and the Department of Agriculture used an early form of the system during the 1960s.[14] As a relatively unknown governor of Georgia, Carter had modified a system originally used at Texas Instruments for the state government. He brought the system to Washington after his inauguration.[15]

ZBB builds a budget from the ground up, through a five-step process:[16]

1. *Define basic "decision units."* The decision unit is the basic building block of the budget. It can be a program, an agency subunit, or project for which a separate budget is prepared.
2. *Build "decision packages" of programs.* Decision packages describe the program's activities and goals. Planners consider different ways of achieving those goals and different levels of activity

in pursuing those goals. For example, planners might develop a minimum-level package, a package budgeted at the previous year's spending, and a package with a significant increase over the previous year. The minimum-level package might be, "maintain entrances at national parks." Additional decision packages might be "open campgrounds," "add environmental educational programs in campgrounds," "operate snack bar for tourists," "construct new hiking trails," and so on.

3. *Rank decision packages.* Agency officials then rank the decision packages in order of priority. National parks officials, for example, might determine that maintaining the entrances to the parks was most important, followed by operating the snack bar, opening the campgrounds, constructing new hiking trails, and adding environmental programs in the campgrounds.

4. *Consolidate the rankings.* At higher levels, officials merge the rankings produced by individual agencies into one overall ranking for the government. For example, they might decide that more money for cleanup of hazardous wastes has higher priority than opening campgrounds in the national parks, which in turn has higher priority than a proposal to increase the number of FBI agents by 5 percent.

5. *Allocate money accordingly.* With the programs arrayed in priority order, decision makers can go down the list until available resources run out. Higher-ranked programs receive money before lower-ranked programs.

In practice, ZBB rarely means budgeting from a zero base. Administrators often have little choice about continuing many programs. Strong political constituencies and congressional pressure would make cutting deeply into many programs impossible. The law, furthermore, often gives administrators little choice. If the Consumer Product Safety Commission discovers that a product is unsafe, it must remove it from the market, regardless of where the product's regulatory oversight program may be ranked in a ZBB system. In the Pentagon, contracts carried over from previous years are legal obligations that must be funded. The sheer workload of ranking all governmental programs from scratch every year, furthermore, would be awesome.

Justifying all programs from the bottom up each year thus is simply impossible—analytically, legally, or politically. Instead, ZBB typically starts with a prescribed minimum level of effort (say, 80 percent of the previous year's allocation) and asks officials to assemble decision packages for increases above this minimum level (say, at 90, 100, and 110 percent of last year's budget). Decision makers consolidate the rankings and fund packages in order until they run out of money.

Therefore, instead of budgeting from a zero base, ZBB in practice means analyzing options at the margins of existing programs. It combines key features of both Wildavsky's political incrementalism and analytical approaches advocating more analysis on the margins of public programs. As in incrementalism, ZBB asks decision makers to consider only small changes to the existing base. As in marginal analysis, it asks decision makers to compare the value of each decision package and rank all of them accordingly. The intention is to impose rational thinking on the incremental process.

As with previous reforms, however, ZBB proved disappointing, for several reasons:[17]

1. *Decision units proved hard to define.* Some agencies established decision units too high in the hierarchy. For these agencies, potential trade-offs became buried within the base. Other agencies established decision units too low in the hierarchy and the agency became overwhelmed with paperwork.

2. *Defining objectives.* Ranking packages is impossible without clear objectives, but objectives often proved too muddy to allow any but the most arbitrary of rankings. Since ZBB grew from the bottom up, lower-level officials developed rankings in the only way they could—based on what they knew. The resulting budget therefore tended to reinforce parochialism because lower-level officials could not see the larger issues the agency faced.[18]

3. *Consolidating packages.* As hard as it was to rank packages at lower levels, the task of consolidating the rankings at higher levels proved even more difficult. The more varied an agency's activities, the more ZBB forced agency officials into "apples and oranges" choices. Which is more important for the Food and Drug Administration: reviewing a new treatment for cancer or reducing the

chances for tampering with drugs? Sometimes budget officials dealt with this problem by not forcing managers to consolidate rankings at high levels, but that of course led to the breakdown of ZBB where it mattered most.

4. *Paperwork*. ZBB produced a flood of paper. In fiscal year 1979, the process produced 25,000 decision packages. When consolidated, OMB faced the chore of ranking 10,000 packages. The volume of the job overwhelmed its participants.

5. *Gamesmanship*. Skillful players soon learned the advantages of reverse rankings. Less-important programs could be protected by building them into the base, while the agency could win increased funding by ranking impossible-to-cut programs very low. Higher-level officials thus would not see how the less-important programs had been safeguarded. They would also feel compelled to grant spending increases to finance politically untouchable programs.

6. *Superficiality*. Many agencies simply grafted ZBB onto their existing budgetary processes. As Allen Schick pointed out, "ZBB could be speedily installed because it did not really change the rules by which budgetary decisions are made." Without clear goals and good performance data, the decision packages became a new arena for playing budgetary games.[19]

On one level, ZBB makes eminent sense. It is, after all, a straightforward attack on V. O. Key's question. It makes much sense to force decision makers to rank proposals for increased funding, rather than put forward a large and disorganized mass of new ideas. In practice, however, as the ranking consolidation process moves up the hierarchy, it becomes ever more impractical. It is one thing to compare marginal changes in national park services. It is more difficult to compare the national parks with environmental protection, and nearly impossible in any reasonable way to consolidate national parks requests with national defense proposals.

Moreover, as the ZBB consolidation process moves into higher levels, decision makers are forced to array their choices without clearly knowing what benefits each alternative would buy. As the decision level rises, the veneer of systematic thinking often remains, but the reality has long since disappeared. In fact, ZBB shares with other analytical budgeting techniques a common problem. Many of these techniques seem simple and useful when applied to an individual's own decisions, or even to the decisions of small organizational units. The higher the level, the more the scale of the problem tends to swamp the technique. At the same time, if agency officials take the technique seriously, the energy required to perform them begins to overwhelm other critical tasks.

Carter was hopeful that ZBB would bring a fresh look at federal spending. Indeed, initial ZBB analysis went far more smoothly than previous budget reforms had. On the other hand, as Schick points out, "The first president to promise a zero base budget . . . delivered the most incremental financial statement since Wildavsky canonized that form of budget-making." Schick argued that Carter's fiscal year 1979 budget was little different than the more traditional process would have produced. In fact, after accounting for inflation, "there appears to have been almost no exercise of presidential power." Most programs were funded at, or slightly above, existing levels.[20] The ZBB process required only superficial adjustments by most federal officials because it did not alter the basic structure of the process. Instead of changing their budgeting techniques to fit ZBB, most agencies adapted ZBB to fit existing techniques. Many agencies became quite skillful in playing the ZBB game.

The Carter administration gradually lost interest in ZBB as time went on. It gave the administration little new leverage over the budget and only encouraged fiscal sleight of hand by agency officials who wrapped "budget outcomes in the pseudo objectivity of numbers,"[21] as Schick put it. Ronald Reagan, David Stockman, and other members of the Reagan administration came into office seeking much more than marginal changes in government programs. While ZBB had considerably greater and more long-lasting success in many state and local governments, where the smaller scale encouraged real ranking of programs, it had a very short life at the federal level.

The Government Performance and Results Act

Faced with declining economic growth, rising government costs, and the need to restore fiscal balance in the late 1970s, the United Kingdom and New Zealand installed radical management and policy reforms. Starting in the late 1970s, for example, New Zealand sold many government-owned services (such as telephone, insurance, airlines, and the post office) to private investors. The government wrote strategic plans that defined what elected wanted officials public programs to accomplish. To achieve these goals, the government gave senior managers much greater flexibility in administering managing programs but also held them far more accountable for the results they achieved. The result, according to many analysts, was a "new public management" centered on six approaches:[22]

1. *Customer service.* The government committed itself to making public services more responsive to citizens' needs.

2. *Operating autonomy.* Government reforms split government functions into smaller, more manageable pieces and gave managers more operating flexibility, especially in budget and human resource policies.

3. *Output measures.* Officials created a results-based measurement system. Agencies and senior managers worked under performance contracts.

4. *Human resources.* The government focused on workforce planning and on strategies to improve motivation of government workers.

5. *Information technology.* To improve service delivery, the government invested substantially in improved information management and computer systems.

6. *Privatization.* Where possible, the government spun public operations off to private owners.

The strategy attracted American reformers. Unlike earlier performance-based systems, it directly tied performance information to budgetary decisions. In providing mangers with more flexibility in exchange for results, reformers hoped that the strategy would provide the incentives missing from earlier attempts to rationalize the process. As part of its "reinventing government" initiative in 1993, the Clinton administration proposed and Congress passed the Government Performance and Results Act. GPRA required all federal agencies to write strategic plans for their activities by 2000. Those plans had to include indicators for measuring their outcomes, so that Congress and OMB alike could assess whether the agencies were achieving their results. Unlike most of the earlier budgetary reforms, Congress invested itself directly in the process by requiring it by law. That made it harder for the effort to melt away or to be abandoned with a shift in presidential administration.

That step alone scarcely guaranteed success. Indeed, many critics complained that GPRA forced a great deal of effort and paperwork on federal agencies in exchange for uncertain results. Cynics dismissed it as yet another in a long line of failed budget reforms—or, worse yet, as an analytical cover for decision to slash some agencies' budgets. However, in a 2002 review of the program, the General Accounting Office (GAO) found that "that agencies continue to tighten the required linkage between their performance plans and budget requests." Agencies' success in writing clear plans varied considerably, GAO found, and "Describing the planned and actual use of resources in terms of measurable results remains an essential action that will continue to require time, adaptation, and effort on the part of all agencies."[23] The work was hard. Getting agreement on program goals, not surprisingly, proved difficult and contentious. Translating those goals into objectives and building good measures for success required skills and strategies not usually seen in government. Political cross-pressures always reared their heads. Given the long and relatively unhappy track record of previous reforms, a healthy measure of cynicism was scarcely surprising.

With its fiscal year 2003 budget proposals, however, the Bush administration used the GPRA process to put political muscle into linking budget goals with management performance. OMB Director Mitch Daniels issued a scathing conclusion about the government's management in concluding, "The federal government is not a well-managed enterprise." To focus attention on the need to improve management—and to connect management results with the budget—the OMB issued a scorecard on five areas: human capital management, competitive sourcing, financial management, electronic government, and linking performance to budgets. OMB then scored each agency in each area through a simple "traffic light" system: a "green light" for success; a "yellow light" for mixed results; and a "red light" for unsatisfactory outcomes. Of 129 grades on the scorecard, 100 were red, 19 were yellow, and just one—for the National Science Foundation's financial management system—was green.[24]

The devastating scorecard ratings got the attention of agency managers and focused substantial attention on GPRA, which to that point had received little public discussion. Whether the scorecards would produce improved performance—and whether performance information would then affect future budget allocations—was anything but clear. Even less clear was whether GPRA would survive the problems that had ultimately crippled other reforms. At the very least, though, it was intriguing for linking performance with the budget and for having the process cemented into law. GRPA's legal sta ding, in fact, helped it survive the transition from President Clinton to President Bush.

Lessons and Truths from the Crusades

The history of budget reform is not a happy one. Few strategies have lasted long, and few have endured changes in presidential administrations. There are, however, several important lessons and enduring truths to be gleaned from this history.

Lessons

Several simple lessons come from the history of attempts to reform the budgetary process:

1. *Success and failure.* Forty years of attempts to rationalize the budgetary process have compiled a record of failure. No strategy has existed in its original form for long, and every administration has officially repudiated the budgetary strategies of the one before it. However, no strategy has ever completely disappeared. Instead, each one has "evaporated," as Richard Rose has put it, leaving behind useful techniques that administrators have continued to use. A survey of municipal governments, conducted in 1987–88, revealed that 45 percent of the municipalities surveyed continued to use ZBB and 70 percent used MBO.[25]

At the federal level, performance budgeting contains simple notions about the relationship of inputs with outputs that endure. The Pentagon still finds the long-term and systems-based planning components of PPBS useful. MBO has left behind a residual of planning that many managers still use. ZBB-style analysis at the margins endures. Even in failure, each technique has produced useful insights that persist.

2. *Political realities: the president.* Several presidents genuinely hoped to improve federal budgeting and management through new budgeting strategies, but no strategy endured for long unless it met the president's immediate needs. The press of political decisions and battles quickly overwhelmed good-government rhetoric. Few initiatives ever work for long without presidential support, and such support has usually quickly waned when the strategy did not prove a magic bullet to slay the bureaucracy or reshape the budget.

3. *Political realities: the Congress.* Most of the strategies, moreover, share a curious feature. They rarely take account of Congress's role in budgeting, and they rarely attempt to restructure programs or decisions in ways that enhance Congress's ability to make decisions. Budgeting is inevitably political, and everything political sooner or later reaches the halls of Congress. Any effort to improve budgeting by making it more analytical but that does not simultaneously meet Congress's needs is doomed to fail. Furthermore, any effort to improve budgeting by making it more managerial tends to emphasize the president over Congress, and that further sows the seeds of budgetary breakdown. Cynics, of course, would ask whether Congress can approach budgeting constructively. The simple fact, however, is that the Constitution mandates an important role for Congress in our budgetary process. The failure of budget reformers to take account of Congress's budgetary role has ensured that none of the reforms would be long lasting.

4. *Bureaucratic realities.* Most of the strategies, furthermore, take little account of how agencies manage and plan their programs. Many of the strategies have encountered difficulties either because they ran in the face of organizational realities (such as PPBS) or because they were easily coopted by them (such as MBO and ZBB). No reform ever lasts long unless those in charge of implementing it see an advantage to themselves in pursuing it. One intriguing feature

of GPRA is that it recognizes this reality and tries to link the performance and budget processes directly.

5. *Predictable cycles.* There is a regular cycle of budgetary
reform.[26] An analyst develops an interesting and useful new approach
to budgeting. To sell the approach to others, its promise is oversold
and it takes on an almost evangelical fervor. Caught up in the potential, policy makers pursue it enthusiastically until they discover that
its results do not match its promise. "Disillusionment sets in," Harry
S. Havens, of the U.S. General Accounting Office, explains, "and we
criticize the new technique for not doing things which intelligent
people should never have expected."[27]

6. *No one tool solves all problems.* In budgetary reform, one size
does not fit all. Rather, the success of reforms has varied, in two ways.
First, the results have varied by the *level* at which budgetary problems have been attacked. Budgeting is very different at the technical
and managerial levels of agencies, in which the agency's mission is
the chief concern, than at higher levels, in which political support
for the agency's activities looms larger. Second, budgetary reform has
also varied with the agency's *output.* Budgeting techniques that work
well for agencies that produce "hard" physical goods with long lives,
such as the Pentagon, often have not worked well for agencies that
produce "soft" services over short periods of time.

Which strategies tended to work best where?

• The logic of performance budgeting has proved attractive to
  managers everywhere, because it encourages a connection
  between resources and outputs. Its guidelines are sufficiently
  vague, however, that it does not always provide a clear guide
  to budgetary decisions.
• PPBS has lasted where the agency's output has been physical,
  on a large scale, with a lasting life. That is why PPBS tended
  to work best in the Pentagon and why its basic precepts endure
  there. It has worked worst where the agency's output has been
  "soft" and service-oriented.
• MBO failed where managers reacted defensively and where it
  did not fit the agency's culture. It worked best in agencies
  where it could help improve existing communication among
  different organizational levels.

- ZBB worked best in support services and worst in agencies that produced physical goods. It also tended to work better at lower levels of agencies, where the task of consolidating rankings was more manageable, than at higher levels, where making analytical trade-offs among disparate programs proved extraordinarily difficult.
- If GPRA works, it will be because it links agency operations and the budgetary process—by linking results with strong incentives to improve them.

Indeed, one cannot truly speak of "success" or "failure" in discussing these reforms. Each one produced important results and at least some lasting effects. Each one, finally, produced some effect simply by forcing managers for a time to think differently about how they budget. Even the most arbitrary or ridiculous reform can sometimes produce positive results by encouraging a fresh look at old problems.

Truths

Budgeting is perhaps the central political act. It is the process of determining who wins and who loses. It is about what programs and values receive society's support. Budgeting is about making choices. Those choices are political, and no rational-analytical approach can ever make it otherwise.

This is not to say, however, that analytical approaches to budgeting are useless or are doomed to failure. Managers often have found some aspects of the reforms useful. They can help identify the critical issues and present information that in turn can persuade political decision makers. Performance budgeting, for example, educates decision makers about what results public spending buys. PPBS allows decision makers to look down the road at the long-range costs for current decisions, and ZBB encourages decision makers to think carefully about changes they are making at the margins of government programs.

As useful as these techniques can in fact be, however, they can never replace the political judgments that lie at the core of budgeting. Any "rational" process can, has, and will be used politically, to the advantage of some and at the expense of others. Different analytical strategies have risen and fallen according to the interests they have served. Thus, rational-analytical techniques tend to last only as long as their political value persists.

The message is simple. Reformers have struggled to help decision makers concentrate on outputs instead of inputs, and on the long term instead of the short term. The reforms have never lived up to the great expectations held for them at their introduction, but none realistically could have done so. Many reforms have at least endured in part. They have lived on where they fit the needs of decision makers at different levels of the system and where they fit the different characteristics of different agencies. Most of all, they have endured where they have helped provide decision makers with information they find useful and timely.

And that might be the most important message of all. Budgetary reform is not a Holy Grail whose elixir mystically replaces conflict with peace. It cannot substitute analysis for politics. At its best, it provides useful information for decision makers as they shape policy.[28] Just how that works, however, varies widely in the budgetary process.

The basic problem that Key asked continues to go without an adequate answer. It can never be answered with purely analytical weapons because his question is fundamentally political, in the best sense of the word. The question can be answered only through the political process because it is, at its core, a political one. Budgeting is about the distribution of taxes and benefits, and few problems are more inherently political.

The failure of these reforms to replace politics with rationality has scarcely kept reformers from trying other approaches. If budgetary analysis cannot do the job, then perhaps changing the budgetary process will. We move to that question next.

Notes

This chapter was originally prepared, in part, under a contract with the U.S. Food and Drug Administration. I am grateful to Gerald L. Barkdoll of FDA, as well as to members of his staff, for extremely helpful suggestions that contributed substantially to the arguments. I am grateful as well for permission to edit and reprint the material here.

1. For a survey of rational and not-so-rational approaches to planning in the United States, see David E. Wilson, *The National Planning Idea in U.S. Public Policy: Five Alternative Approaches* (Boulder, Colo.: Westview Press, 1980).
2. V. O. Key, "The Lack of a Budgetary Theory," *American Political Science Review* 34 (December 1940): 1137.
3. Charles E. Lindblom, "The Science of Muddling Through," *Public Administration Review* 19 (Spring 1959): 79–88.
4. Aaron Wildavsky, *The Politics of the Budgetary Process* (Boston: Little, Brown, 1964).
5. For a history and description of performance budgeting, see Jesse Burkhead, *Government Budgeting* (New York: John Wiley, 1956), esp. Chapters 6 and 7.
6. Unpublished memorandum, quoted by Burkhead, *Government Budgeting*, p. 142.
7. Ibid., pp. 153–4.
8. For an examination of the issues and the case for PPBS, see Charles J. Hitch and Roland McKean, *The Economics of Defense in the Nuclear Age* (Cambridge: Harvard University Press, 1967). Charles L. Schultze has an enthusiastic endorsement of the approach in *The Politics and Economics of Public Spending* (Washington: Brookings Institution, 1968). Finally, for a history of the development of PPBS, see Robert D. Lee, Jr., and Ronald W. Johnson, *Public Budgeting Systems* (Baltimore: University Park Press, 1983).
9. Lee and Johnson, *Public Budgeting Systems*, p. 99.
10. Frederick C. Mosher and John E. Harr, *Programming Systems and Foreign Policy Leadership* (New York: Oxford University Press, 1970), p. 206.
11. Richard Rose, "Implementation and Evaporation: The Record of MBO," *Public Administration Review* 37 (January/February 1977): 66. See also Richard Rose, *Managing Presidential Objectives* (New York: Free Press, 1976); and Lee and Johnson, *Public Budgeting Systems*, pp. 113–14.
12. This discussion draws from Rose, "Implementation and Evaporation," pp. 67–8.
13. Richard Rose, "Implementation and Evaporation: The Record of MBO," *Public Administration Review* 37 (January/February 1977), esp. pp. 67–8.

14. Lawrence A. Gordon and Donna M. Heivilin, "Zero-Base Budgeting in the Federal Government: An Historical Perspective," *GAO Review* 13 (Fall 1978): 57–65.
15. For a discussion of Phyrr's techniques, see his "Zero-Base Budgeting," *Harvard Business Review* 48 (November/December 1970): 111–21; and *Zero-Base Budgeting: A Practical Tool for Evaluating Expenses* (New York: John Wiley and Sons, 1973).
16. See Gordon and Heivilin, "Zero-Base Budgeting," and Lee and Johnson, *Public Budgeting Systems*, pp. 116–22.
17. Scott S. Cowen, "ZBB—Where and How It Has Worked," *Business Horizons* 29 (May/June 1979): 50.
18. Frank D. Draper and Bernard T. Pitsvada, "ZBB—Looking Back after Ten Years," *Public Administration Review* 41 (January/February 1981): 79.
19. Allen Schick, "The Road from ZBB," *Public Administration Review* 38 (March/April 1978): 178.
20. Ibid., p. 177.
21. Ibid., p. 178.
22. See Sandford Borins, "What the New Public Management Is Achieving: A Survey of Commonwealth Experience," in Lawrence R. Jones, Kuno Schedler, and Stephen W. Wade, eds., *Advances in International Comparative Public Management* (Greenwich, Corn.: JAI Press, 1997), p. 65. More generally, see Donald F. Kettl, *The Global Public Management Revolution: A Report on the Transformation of Governance* (Washington: Brookings, 2000).
23. U.S. General Accounting Office, *Managing for Results: Agency Progress in Linking Performance Plans with Budgets and Financial Statements*, Report 02–236 (January 2002), p. 3.
24. See Tom Shoop, "Bush's Budget Rips Agency Management in Key Areas," Govexec.com (February 4, 2002), at http://www.govexec.com/dailyfed/0202/020402ts1.htm (last accessed February 12, 2002).
25. Theodore H. Poister and Gregory Streib, "Management Tools in Municipal Government: Trends over the Past Decade," *Public Administration Review* 49 (May/June 1989): 240–8.
26. Harry S. Havens, "Looking Back at PPBS: Image vs. Substance," *GAO Review* 12 (Winter 1977): 10–15. More broadly, see Allen Schick, "The Road to PPB: The Stages of Budget Reform," *Public Administration Review* 26 (December 1966): 243–58.
27. Havens, ibid., p. 10.
28. For an examination of this phenomenon in one reform, see Havens, ibid., p. 13.

CHAPTER 5

Fixing the Process

Even casual observers realize that budgeting has increasingly become caught in stalemate. Conflicts have multiplied, delays have increased, recriminations have grown—and the deficits have scarcely disappeared. Presidents have often blamed Congress for the problems. Members of Congress have replied that presidents too often submitted budgets that have been declared DOA, dead on arrival, because they could never be passed as written. Budgeting has frequently seemed a game of maneuvering for political advantage, for casting blame, instead of reaching the key decisions about the nation's money. Budget analysts have questioned whether the government any longer retains "the capacity to budget."[1]

Because elected officials and the institutions in which they work seem unable to make the tough decisions, reformers have suggested instead that it is the budget *process* that needs to be reformed. They seek to alter the process to help budget makers make decisions they would prefer to avoid. They seek to provide political cover behind which the tough decisions can be made. They seek ways of tying both the president and the Congress, both Democrats and Republicans, to the results so that no one can seize political advantage from the inevitable fallout. In short, through reforms both tried and suggested, reformers have attempted to substitute process for politics.

Procedural Problems

For years, reformers have debated fixes for the budget's procedural problems. Despite the debates and several significant changes, important problems remain.

105

Delays

Most embarrassing are the continual delays in putting the budget together. With regular precision, the beginning of the new federal fiscal year approaches each October 1. The president and Congress haggle and maneuver and, usually, do not finish their work on time. Duels between the president and Congress have often brought new budgetary years without a new budget in place. In fact, from 1975 to 1990 Congress and the president managed to agree on all thirteen appropriations bills before October 1 only twice, in fiscal years 1977 and 1989. In fiscal 1977, Congress and the president actually managed to get their work done on time, just before the 1976 presidential election. The October 1987 stock market crash panicked budget makers, for news accounts repeatedly warned them that the financial community saw the absence of a plan to reduce the deficit as a sign of real weakness in the economy. A special postcrash budget summit put together the budget for both fiscal years 1988 and 1989 at the same time. The summit was long after the beginning of fiscal year 1988, but it did pave the way for a relatively peaceful fiscal 1989 budget process. The agreement had an important side benefit: it swept the budget debate out of the way until after the 1988 presidential election. During the 1990s, the situation was little better. Congress beat the start of the new fiscal year only twice from 1990 through 2001—and then just by a day. On average, the budget was 50 days late in being passed (see Figure 5–1).

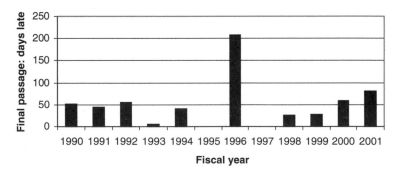

Figure 5–1 Delays in the Congressional Budget Process

Before 1977, the federal government's *fiscal year* began on July 1. However, Congress had such difficulty in completing its work before the new year started that it pushed fiscal year's starting date back to October 1. The extra three months has made little difference—the budget is now as late as (or later than) it ever was before the change.

Everyone complains about not meeting the time schedules, but no one seems to have a cure. The recurring failure to make a budget embarrasses everyone involved. In the worst disputes, the president and Congress have been unable to agree even on a "continuing resolution" (which keeps the wheels turning temporarily until a budget can be passed). Without money, the government just shuts down, from the panda house at the National Zoo to thousands of federal office buildings around the country. The shutdowns, furthermore, actually cost the government money, since there is considerable expense in all of the procedures required. The shutdown over Columbus Day weekend in 1990 cost the government $1.7 million.[2] A series of shutdowns in late 1995 led to hundreds of thousands of federal workers to being told to stay home and to a tension-filled standoff between President Clinton and House of Representatives Speaker Newt Gingrich. It is bad enough, in the eyes of most observers, that the government does not seem to be able to govern. It is worse that such ungovernability adds to the cost of the problems.

Institutional and Partisan Conflict

Recurring budget battles have also worsened relations between the presidency and the Congress and, within Congress, between Republicans and Democrats. They have even frequently spilled over into intraparty squabbles. The failure to reach agreement on the budget immobilizes key fiscal decisions. The distrust and cynicism, the maneuvers and the bickering, affect not only the budget but also all policy making that requires joint work by the two branches. If congressional Democrats suspect the president's negotiators of dealing from the bottom of the deck in budget negotiations, they might well distrust him on other issues. Budget battles can run over into disputes concerning Supreme Court nominations, environmental legislation, foreign policy, and ultimately political campaigns.

No dispute in Washington can be compartmentalized. Anyone who loses a battle on one front is sorely tempted to take up arms on another. Sincere negotiations between the president and the Congress are more difficult when a bitter taste remains from budget struggles. Bipartisan policy making is far harder when Democrats and Republicans distrust one another from earlier budget skirmishes. It is even harder for party leaders in the Congress to keep the members of their own party in line when those members fear that their campaign promises can be undercut by deals hammered out in closed sessions among a small group of leaders. Party members sometimes feel that the only way to protect themselves is to separate their position from the party's, and that only increases the deterioration of party discipline so prevalent in Washington politics.

Hard Decisions

Lingering behind these problems is a clear sense among many observers that the answers to the budget dilemma are right under our noses—but that elected officials do not have the guts to make them. For some, the answer is to reduce government expenses to meet income. In this view, the problem is that the government is simply spending too much money, and the key is to cut programs. The deficit thus is the result of unsound financial planning. For others, the answer is to increase taxes to meet society's demand. These observers argue that we are a rich country with many serious needs that only government can meet. The deficit thus is an artificial construct that should not limit government's role. For yet others, the answer is to spur the economy along, so that there is more room for higher spending while taxes go up even faster. The deficit, in this view, is an element in an even broader political-economic strategy.

The Gramm-Rudman Fix

Whether because the system punishes those who dare to try, or whether more cynically it is because elected officials lack courage, many observers believe that elected officials resist making the hard decisions. The answer, they say, is to create a budget process that will make it easier to make the tough decisions that will provide a smoke screen behind which deals can be struck to supply political backbone for those who lack it. In short, reformers seek to replace the problems of *political* decision making with a *process* that will produce the decisions automatically instead.

Gramm-Rudman I

Congress tried to do just that, in 1985, with the Balanced Budget and Emergency Deficit Control Act—Gramm-Rudman, for short. Senators Phil Gramm (R-Tex.), Warren Rudman (R-N.H.), and Ernest F. Hollings (D-S.C.) argued that the recurring battles without results ought to end. They framed a process steered by an automatic pilot to balance the budget within five years, by fiscal year 1991. (The act was known at first as Gramm-Rudman-Hollings. Capital comics argued that cuts had to be made everywhere, and soon it became simply Gramm-Rudman.) Declining deficit targets were set for each of the five years. If the budget deficit were projected to exceed that target, Congress and the president could seek agreement on a way to cut spending, increase taxes, or both so that the target would be met. If agreement proved impossible, then automatic cuts, half from national defense and half from domestic programs, would do the job instead. By the fifth year, the deficit would reach zero.

The principal of Gramm-Rudman seemed simple and foolproof. The act established a clear goal with specific intermediate targets. It created a specter of automatic cuts so terrible that making the hard decisions would be preferable. And, if that proved impossible, the automatic cuts would kick in and do the job instead. No one, including the bill's supporters, thought the idea was a good one. Senator Rudman, in fact, called it "a bad idea whose time has come."[3] To a majority of both houses of Congress and the Reagan administration, however, it seemed better than anything else, especially the conventional political approach to the budget. If the act's incentives failed to reduce the deficit, the automatic cutting process was always a gun behind the door.[4]

Before Gramm-Rudman's friends had a chance to put the act to the test, the Supreme Court declared a key portion unconstitutional.

Under the act, the General Accounting Office (GAO) was in charge of defining and enforcing the cuts, but the Supreme Court held that GAO, as part of the legislative branch, could not perform executive functions, such as ordering cuts in the executive branch. Almost immediately, Gramm-Rudman was rendered toothless. Congress and President Reagan began negotiating on a fix.

Gramm-Rudman II

Congress corrected the constitutional problem in 1987, by reluctantly agreeing to change the act's enforcer from GAO to the president's Office of Management and Budget (OMB). Moving the enforcement machinery to the executive branch solved the constitutional problem, but it also worried congressional Democrats. So long as the presidency was controlled by the Republicans, the OMB would be able to slight their interests, the Democrats worried. No other alternative seemed constitutional, however, so they reluctantly accepted OMB's role. In the process, Democratic congressional leaders wrote the Gramm-Rudman amendment in a way that gave OMB relatively little discretion in how the cuts would be applied.

More important, Congress and the president made the annual deficit targets easier to reach. After just two years, it was already clear that the original Gramm-Rudman schedule was far too ambitious, and that it would be impossible to balance the budget by fiscal year (FY) 1991. They agreed on a three-step reform. First, they agreed to stretch out the timetable for eliminating the deficit, from FY 1991 to FY 1993. Second, they postponed any truly painful decisions until after the 1988 presidential election by making the targets for the next two budgets much easier to reach. Third, after the 1988 presidential election, they put Gramm-Rudman back on the slope set in the original act. This combination, they hoped, would avoid the immediate political battles that would have come with tough Gramm-Rudman cuts in a presidential election year while keeping to the spirit of the original act. Their hopes were quickly dashed again, however. The deficit proved stubborn and, by 1990, it began moving up sharply even as the deficit targets were moving down.

Running in Place

Put together, the successive versions of Gramm-Rudman were a story of titanic struggles, often with few accomplishments. Never before, to borrow liberally from Britain's wartime prime minister, Winston Churchill, had so many struggled so long and produced so little. Debate over each new Gramm-Rudman revision sparked fierce political battles. Each year, both congressional leaders and the president had pledged themselves to hitting the Gramm-Rudman targets. At the end of most years, however, a balanced budget seemed still distant and the task for the following year even greater. Working through the Gramm-Rudman process became like walking up a down escalator. There was a great deal of motion and effort, but progress always seemed fleeting.

What happened? Gramm-Rudman, after all, seemed in all of its versions to have an inescapable logic. Annual targets were clear. If Congress and the president could not agree on how to meet the targets, automatic cuts would kick in to do the job instead. One way or another, there thus would be a steady reduction in the deficit, and each year's success would set the stage for more reductions the next year. The deficit proved very uncooperative, however. Over the life of Gramm-Rudman I and II, the deficit never hit its target. What happened?

1. Gramm-Rudman targets used "snapshots." The critical calculations about each year's budget deficit were "snapshots" taken near the beginning of the fiscal year. What mattered was the deficit estimate on the day it was taken. Changes, either legislative or economic, that later changed the deficit simply did not matter. Thus, if the key scorekeepers produced a budget that, in their estimation, hit the targets, the cuts were avoided. The process created enormous incentives for choosing the projections that minimized the current year's pain, while postponing difficult decisions until later. When later came, the problem repeated. Each year seemed to suggest progress, but the deficit reductions were often more cosmetic than real.

2. Much of the budget was untouched by Gramm-Rudman. From the very beginning, Congress and the president had agreed to make nearly 70 percent of the federal budget exempt from the across-the-board cuts. Interest on the debt had to be paid, and Gramm Rudman's supporters argued that cuts should not be imposed on recipients or social security benefits or of veterans' retirement payments. They also agreed to spare welfare and several other domestic programs. Only about 30 percent of the budget remained after accounting for the exemptions. If the Gramm-Rudman axe fell, it cut far more deeply in some programs, such as air-traffic control or defense contract management, than in others. The fiscal 1988 cuts, for example, took 10.5 percent from the defense programs subject to Gramm-Rudman and 8.5 percent from nondefense programs. The very severity of these cuts created enormous incentives to avoid them.

   3. *Small changes in economic estimates dramatically changed deficit estimates.* Each year, the budget included assumptions about the nation's economic health that affected the deficit projections. Each year, decision makers seized on overoptimistic economic projections that reduced the size of the projected deficit. (We will shortly explore this problem.) And each year, reality did not cooperate; for example, in fiscal 1990, the deficit jumped in just a few weeks to more than $12 billion above the target, as the economy weakened. Budget makers found it very attractive to use the most hopeful economic assumptions that seemed reasonable. The economy never seemed to cooperate, however. The deficit proved remarkably stubborn and each year tended to leave budget makers with a bigger problem than that of the year before.

   4. *Budget makers often relied on "blue smoke and mirrors."* A vast number of shell games can produce apparent savings while doing nothing in the long run about the deficit. In 1989, for example, budget makers agreed to change the Pentagon's payday from the first day of the month to the last day of the month. Checks that would have been distributed on fiscal 1990 new year's day, October 1, 1989 (and counted against the fiscal 1990 deficit) were distributed instead on the last day of fiscal 1989, September 30. The government thus *reduced* the FY 1990 deficit by billions of dollars and made the job of hitting the Gramm-Rudman targets for the year that much easier. The deficit for FY 1989, of course, was *increased* by the exact same amount, but for Gramm-Rudman purposes this did not matter. The

"snapshot" for the fiscal 1989 deficit had been taken a year before, and changes made after that snapshot did not matter. The result: absolutely no real effect on the government's financial condition, but apparent progress in reducing the deficit.[5] Deficit politics has made budget makers remarkably clever and inventive. They have become quite skilled at using the blue smoke and mirrors of magicians to create the illusion of deficit reduction, often without doing anything real.

5. *The big expenditures were hidden from the process.* Along the Gramm-Rudman path, big policy problems emerged. Hundreds of the nation's savings and loan associations went under, and the federal government launched a huge bailout. The ultimate cost of the bailout is truly unknown, but GAO analysts worried that the total might reach $500 billion—$2000 for every man, woman, and child in the country. Some of these expenditures were hidden from the deficit through a maze of complicated borrowing programs. The costs were real, but their effects on the deficit were minimized by accounting decisions.

Gramm-Rudman III

When President Bush submitted his budget for fiscal year 1991 to Congress in February 1990, he projected that he could meet the Gramm-Rudman II target (a $64 billion deficit)—if Congress agreed to the policy changes he recommended. Within months, however, his hope disappeared. In the midst of the budget summit, a souring economy pushed the deficit projection up to nearly $300 billion. Finding a political compromise to bring the deficit down to the $64 billion target was impossible. The $230 billion in across-the-board cuts that the Gramm-Rudman process would have produced were too terrible even to contemplate. The air-traffic control system would have been immobilized, the FBI would have been decimated, federal prisons would have been desperately shorthanded, and similar problems would have multiplied throughout the government. Yet another Gramm-Rudman "fix" was needed.

As part of the 1990 budget summit, President Bush and Congress agreed to abandon the 1987 targets set by Gramm-Rudman II in 1987. They moved instead to a new deficit-reduction system, with far more modest targets enforced by an extremely complicated system:[6]

1. Limits for discretionary spending. The budget negotiators began by separating mandatory spending—for entitlements and interest on the debt (about two thirds of total spending)—from discretionary spending (about one third of the total). The discretionary programs (that is, programs controlled by annual appropriations) were then divided into three categories. First were defense programs, which include the activities administered by the program as well as defense-related functions conducted in other agencies, such as the manufacture of nuclear weapons in the Department of Energy. Second were international programs, which includes foreign aid. Finally, there were domestic programs, which include everything from space and environmental programs to transportation programs and the basic conduct of government.

The 1990 reform set separate spending ceilings for each of these categories for the first three years of the new process, FY 1991, 1992, and 1993. The targets held defense spending nearly constant and allowed domestic spending to grow slightly. International programs were held even, but they amounted to only a small share of the discretionary programs: only 4 percent of all discretionary spending, and just 1.5 percent of total spending. For 1994 and 1995, the reform established overall ceilings for discretionary spending.

2. A new "pay-as-you-go" system for mandatory spending programs and revenues. The negotiators then moved to mandatory programs, such as social security, medicare, and military and civilian retirement. Any changes considered for any mandatory program or for taxes must be "deficit-neutral"; that is, on balance they must not increase or decrease the deficit. The general plan was christened "pay-as-you-go," since taxes could not be cut or entitlements increased so long as equivalent savings were found. Social security was subject to a slightly different pay-as-you-go rule. The negotiators built what they called a "firewall" between social security and the rest of the budget to prevent tampering with the social security surplus. The social security program's finances were completely separated from all other deficit calculations under Gramm-Rudman III, so the program would not be drawn into disputes in the rest of the budget over how to meet the spending ceilings. Special rules in each house of Congress required unusual majorities to consider provisions that might reduce the social security surplus. Separate rules were also established for deposit insurance in commercial banks, which became a major spending item as banks weakened in the early 1990s.

3. *Backing away from specific deficit targets.* The overall deficit targets of Gramm-Rudman I and II proved to be the source of much mischief, as budget negotiators developed remarkable ways to hit the targets without making real long-term deficit reductions. The summitteers abandoned the promise of eliminating the deficit and instead set a far more modest objective of an $83 billion deficit for fiscal 1985 instead. That change, more than anything else, recognized just how difficult the job of reducing the deficit truly was.

4. *Bringing credit programs into the budget.* When budgets were tight, budget makers frequently had found it attractive to spend money through federal direct loan and loan guarantee programs, such as federally guaranteed student loans. (In a direct loan program, such as housing assistance, the federal government itself lends money to a borrower. In a guaranteed loan program, such as student loan programs, borrowers obtain money from private institutions, such as banks, and the federal government promises to repay the money if the borrower does not. The federal government frequently supplies a subsidy with guaranteed loans as well.) Rarely were the full costs of these programs included on the budget, so expensive programs could be enacted without the appearance that the federal government was committing much money. The 1990 reforms required that the full cost of direct loans or guaranteed loans be recorded on the budget when the loans are made. These costs were to be included in the ceilings for each budget category and were subject to the pay-as-you-go requirements.

5. *Providing new enforcement procedures.* Under the 1990 act, Congress would not be allowed to make program changes that exceeded the ceilings established in the law. Furthermore, if any of the three budget categories for the discretionary budget—defense, international programs, or domestic programs—threatened to exceed their ceilings, automatic across-the-board cuts would bring spending back under the ceilings. These cuts applied only to programs within that category, however. Thus, if defense spending were estimated to

exceed the ceiling, across-the-board cuts would be applied, but only for defense programs. Domestic and international programs would not be affected. After years of squabbling over defense versus domestic programs, Congress and the president agreed to enforce cuts only on the part of the budget that exceeded its ceiling.

6. Making OMB the scorekeeper. A major issue in Gramm-Rudman III was who would be in charge of keeping score within each of the categories. The Democratic negotiators agreed to give that role to the president's OMB. Scorekeeping determined whether programs were meeting their ceilings or not, so the agreement substantially increased OMB's power.

Unlike the earlier versions, Gramm-Rudman III was built on a more-solid foundation. The economic assumptions built within it were ambitious, but not as unrealistic as the previous versions. The targets in the budgetary categories themselves were relatively realistic. Rudolph G. Penner, former director of the Congressional Budget Office, wrote that the change "brought forth the most important and most honest deficit-reduction package seen for a very long time."[7] If Congress and the president held themselves to the agreements they had reached—and if they made the cuts implicit in the targets they had set—a significant reduction in the deficit seemed inevitable. The problem, of course, was the "if." Immediately after the end of the war against Iraq, Pentagon officials began wondering out loud if the ceilings would allow them to maintain the kind of postwar forces that seemed needed. Pulling on one thread of the agreement threatened to unravel it all. The agreement was fragile and open to new negotiations. Budget experts concluded, however, that the agreement itself was a more solid foundation on which to work and that if Congress and the president held themselves to the agreement, real deficit reductions would follow.

Other Reform Ideas

Gramm-Rudman, launched with great expectations in an apparently leakproof boat, proved disappointing. To be sure, it did genuinely reduce the deficit a bit. Budget makers had to confront the overall effect of what they were doing on the deficit. The process also increasingly made it impossible for anyone to propose new programs without suggesting a way to pay for them. The overall results of Gramm-Rudman, however, were very modest and, as budget analyst Lawrence J. Haas points out, "any deficit cutting accomplished by Gramm-Rudman has come at great cost to the integrity of government."[8] One of the nation's leading budget experts, Henry J. Aaron from the Brookings Institution, lamented, "I have the sense that as Congress and the administration are forced to go through these exercises and resort to such devices, that we are all performing childish rituals rather than engaging in adult debate about constructive national policy."[9] The many failures of Gramm-Rudman led to other suggestions for reform of the budgetary process.

Line-Item Veto

President Reagan regularly asked Congress for a line-item veto. If governors in forty-three states could refuse to approve individual pieces (line items) of spending bills, he argued, the president ought to have that power, too. President Reagan promised that if he had that power, he could wield it to reduce federal spending substantially. In 1988, in fact, he promised to reveal a list of the programs he would cut if given a chance. His budget analysts were taken aback by the promise, and they tried for weeks to duck having to produce the list. Finally, when pressed, they came up with a list of $1.5 billion in cuts that, they said, President Reagan would have made if he could exercise the line-item veto. The reduction was just 1 percent of the $150 billion deficit that year, and only about 0.001 percent of the entire federal budget.

One might argue on constitutional grounds that the president ought to have greater power to disapprove spending for individual federal programs. The Founders chose to allow the president authority to approve or veto only entire pieces of legislation. Simply because they wrote the Constitution that way, it need not remain in that form forever. It does mean, however, that any discussion of the line-item veto has to be considered from the much broader perspective of the balance of power between Congress and the president, and not just as a deficit-reduction tactic. Congress has obviously been unwilling to consider yielding such authority to the president, and it is unlikely to approve the constitutional amending that would be required to give the president the power.

Even if Congress were willing, however, it is unlikely that the line-item veto would ever be of much use to presidents in reducing the deficit. Most of the programs on the list President Reagan produced in 1988 were small pork-barrel projects that were very important to individual members of Congress. Often such projects are the glue that holds together congressional compromises and the deals that presidents strike with members of Congress. If the president were to line-item veto such a project, it would be unlikely that the member whose district was affected would ever work with the president again. If the president were to promise to veto all such projects, the loss of this glue of compromise would make it far harder to produce key legislative packages.

Whatever sense the line-item veto might make, its importance clearly is not economic. Its potential for reducing the deficit, especially when such a huge part of the budget is uncontrollable, is modest indeed. Its potential for political fallout is enormous. The real importance of the line-item veto is as a political weapon that could be used selectively by the president in bargaining with Congress. It is a tool to shift the balance of power. Members of Congress realize that it is a political-constitutional issue, not an economic one, and naturally seek to defend their branch's power from executive encroachment.

Balanced-Budget Amendment

A constitutional amendment to require Congress and the president to produce a balanced budget is another popular remedy. If the problem is the lack of political will, then a constitutional amendment could supply the needed backbone, the argument goes. There might be a phase-in period over several years, during which the deficit would be gradually reduced to zero. After that, the budget would have to be balanced every year.

Such a proposal might very well create a budget that, at least on paper, is balanced, but it would undoubtedly create a great deal of mischief as well. The easiest way to comply with such a requirement is simply to define new programs, especially expensive new programs, as "off-budget" entities that would not affect the budget. No major war in the nation's history, for example, has been financed with a balanced budget. The nation in every case has had to run big deficits and borrow substantial sums of money (or, in the case of the war with Iraq, request support from the nation's allies). It would be tempting to hide important programs, big and small, from deficit calculations, just as Congress and the president agreed to do for the savings-and-loan bailout and the war with Iraq.

Even if some way were found to force budget makers to account for the costs of all government programs, even defining what "balance" means is deceptively difficult. The notion seems simple: Expenditures ought not exceed revenues. The experience in state governments, which must balance their budgets each year, shows just how hard it is in practice to enforce the norm of balance. There are endless strategies and tactics to produce a budget that, at least is the short term, is in balance—and that in the long run can show big deficits. Establishing such a rule simply creates enormous incentives to find ways around it. Students play with margins, spacing, type styles, and other parts of a term paper to make it come out to the length that the instructor expects. Budget makers, with far more experience and much more at stake, can be infinitely more creative. A "balanced" budget can be produced, but that does not necessarily produce a long-run balance of government revenues and expenditures.

Biennial Budget

If budget makers cannot produce a budget in one year's time, why not allow them to make two year's budgets at once? Members of the administration and of Congress alike complain that they have virtually no time for anything but budgeting. No sooner is the previous year's crisis over than it is time to start again. Why not enact, in the first year of each two-year session of Congress, a budget to cover both years? That way, at least one year would be relatively clear to do other work. Modest changes could be made to take account of new circumstances, but each new year at least would not force open yet another new can of worms.

In fact, since 1987 the Pentagon has been submitting biennial budgets, covering its estimates for programs over a two-year period. Congress has resisted moving any further, however. Congressional leaders worry that dealing with the changes through supplemental appropriations bills would still occupy an enormous amount of time—and that, in the meantime, they would be deprived of a fresh look at the whole package. They worry, as well, that working on a two-year basis would transfer enormous power to the president and his budget staff, who would inevitably have much more discretion over the details of the budget. Finally, economic estimates have tended to upset the best-negotiated plans. Economic forecasting for just one year is frequently a risky business. Basing a budget on a two-year forecast is far more uncertain, and the pressures for reopening the debate if the deficit moved significantly up or down would be inevitable. This strategy, like the others, is far more important for the way it shifts power among budget makers than for its potential for reducing the deficit.

Forecasting Taxes and Spending

A recurring theme in the earlier sections of this chapter is the important role that economic forecasting plays in budgeting. A strong economy reduces the deficit, and a weak economy drives it up. The task of forecasting economic performance thus lies at the core of the budget's process problems.

Other things being equal, the stronger the economy—that is, the higher the level of economic growth and the lower the levels of unemployment and inflation—the lower will be the deficit. High economic growth tends to put people to work. Productively employed workers contribute more in taxes, so revenues increase. They also demand fewer governmental services, such as unemployment compensation, food stamps, and medicaid. High economic growth thus cuts the growth of spending compared with what it might have been, increases revenues, and overall cuts the deficit. Conversely, when unemployment rises or inflation increases, the deficit tends to increase. Fewer workers are contributing less tax revenue, and the demand for government services pushes spending up. Inflation, moreover, often drives expenses up faster than do tax revenues.

The dynamics of budget forecasting create two important incentives for budget makers. First, it is obviously in everyone's interest to encourage the strongest possible economic growth. This is not always easy to do because, with deficits so persistently high, policy makers have lost most of their ability to steer the economy through the budget. Nearly all of the burden of economic management has fallen instead to the Federal Reserve, which has its hands full balancing a complex array of different, and often competing forces. Nevertheless, everyone seeks sustained economic expansion. Among many other positive results, it makes budgetary politics easier.

Second, it is also makes budgetary politics easier if budget makers can *project* strong economic growth. Most observers focus on presidential-congressional negotiators as the core of budgetary politics, but budgeting really builds on economic projections. Budget makers fight over *estimates*: estimates of how much money is likely to flow into the government through taxes; estimates of how much money will flow out of the government through entitlements, existing commitments, and new programs. When congressional or administration negotiators debate over what the deficit for the next year will be, they are really struggling over deficit estimates. They can never know precisely what expenditures or revenues will be until long after the fiscal year is over. All they can focus on, therefore, are the best guesses of analysts about the implications of different strategies.

The Importance of Forecasting

Over the last thirty years, the importance of economic forecasting for budgetary politics has increased enormously, for several reasons:

1. Economic instability. In recent decades, the economy has gone through two wars, in Vietnam and in Iraq; two major oil shocks; stagflation, with simultaneous high inflation and high unemployment; several recessions of varying severity; a rapidly escalating federal debt burden; and the growth of a global economy in which no nation can act alone. All these factors have increased economic uncertainty, and each of them has affected the federal budget in important and sometimes unanticipated ways. Attempting to forecast their economic effects has become far more important to decision makers struggling to gain control over the budget.

2. *Entitlements.* As the share of the budget devoted to entitlements has risen, so too has the importance of forecasting how large entitlement spending will be. Once created, entitlement programs such as social security and medicare take on a life of their own. Next year's outlays for social security, for example, will be shaped by how many new individuals will become eligible for social security payments; how many existing beneficiaries will die; how many existing beneficiaries will continue receiving checks; and how much each beneficiary will be eligible to receive each month, according to the complex formula used to compute benefits. This is a difficult forecast because of the many variables involved, but it is within the limits of modern computer power. Only computer experts, however, can produce the projections that the budget makers need.

3. *Tax reform.* Over the last twenty years, budget makers have been even more eager than previously to "reform," in nearly every sense of that word, the tax code. They have tried to encourage economic growth through lower tax rates. They have attempted to stabilize the social security system by increasing the payroll tax. They have given and taken away from local governments incentives to build sports arenas through special tax breaks, and they have given and taken away from individuals inducements to insulate their homes. The catalog of tax changes is lengthy, and every modification affects tax receipts. In the 1990 tax summit, for example, congressional and administration negotiators battled over whether President Bush's plan to lower the tax rate for capital gains would increase or decrease tax revenues. Again, computer analysts worked overtime to generate their best guesses.

4. *Budget reform.* The budget reforms of the 1970s and 1980s achieved little progress in reducing the deficit. Each one, however, has pushed budget makers toward accounting for the effects of their decisions for total expenditures, revenues, and the deficit. Before 1974, for example, neither Congress nor the president had strong incentives to confront the totals after the president sent his budget to Capitol Hill. After the 1974 Congressional Budget Act, and increasing with every budget reform since, budget makers have been

forced to calculate and recalculate the totals as well as individual parts of the budget. That effort, in turn, has called for more computer power.

5. *The spread of computers.* If calculating the totals is important, so too is *whose* calculations are used. During most of the 1980s, Republicans used their projections of high deficits to restrain Democrats' plans for domestic programs. Democrats did likewise to reduce President Reagan's defense buildup. Both sides have searched for optimistic economic projections when ducking the issue during presidential election years was attractive. In 1990, OMB's projections showed that the president's capital gains tax reduction would bring more money in, while congressional Democrats produced numbers that showed a long-run reduction in revenues. Whose projections are used heavily shapes the nature of the battle. The computers, programs, and databases have become so widely available that most of the key players can now produce their own projections. Budget negotiations therefore have become battles not only over programs but also over competing economic forecasts.

How Are Projections Made?

Forecasts of federal expenditures and receipts, and therefore of the deficit, are the result of what analysts call *econometric models*. Extremely sophisticated models of the economy contain hundreds of different features, ranging from detailed estimates of production in different parts of the economy, the level of interest rates, the amount of foreign trade, the degree of inflation, and how high unemployment will be. High-speed computers make relatively short work of crunching all of the numbers and produce estimates of the different parts of the government's financial picture. Econometric analysis is sufficiently advanced that different models themselves produce very similar results. What makes forecasts differ is the set of assumptions about economic performance that analysts put into them.

The government's forecasts have been criticized for widely and regularly missing the mark. In one sense, these forecasts have paradoxically proven remarkably good. From 1982 through 1999, the Congressional Budget Office, the administration, and private economic forecasters all tended to underestimate growth by small and

Table 5–1   Sensitivity of Budget to Economic Assumptions

Effect of	Effect on surplus (+) or deficit (−) for fiscal year 2002	Effect on surplus (+) or deficit (−) for fiscal years 2003–2012
	(dollar amounts in billions)	
1% lower growth in GDP for 2002 only	−11.5	−394.1
1% lower growth in GDP each year 2002–2012 (no change in unemployment)	−9.4	−1901.1
1% higher rate of inflation and interest rates for 2002 only	+2.2	+106.2
1% higher rate of inflation and interest rates for 2002–2012	+2.3	+783.9

Source: Office of Management and Budget, *Budget of the United States Government, Fiscal Year 2003: Analytical Perspectives* (GPO, 2002), p. 30.

relatively similar amounts: 0.7 percent for CBO, 0.5 percent for the administration, and 0.8 percent for private forecasters.[10] In statistical terms, the differences are negligible, but the political results have been enormous because minor statistical modeling errors produce huge differences in the deficit estimates. For example, as Table 5–1 shows, just a 1 percent error in forecasting economic growth or inflation can have a significant effect on deficit projections for the coming year—and a huge impact when compounded across a decade. The further into the future analysts attempt to make projections, the more even small errors matter. Two budget experts, Rudolph B. Penner and Alan J. Abramson, explain:

> Changing a deficit estimate by $10 billion by changing an economic forecast is a minor statistical event. Changing policies sufficiently to alter a deficit estimate by $10 billion is a significant political event. This asymmetry creates an enormous temptation to achieve a given deficit target

by adopting optimistic economic assumptions rather than by cutting programs or raising taxes. It is little wonder that the economic forecast adopted by Congress for the purpose of formulating the first budget resolution [Congress's initial annual vote on the budget] was too optimistic on balance every year in FY 1980–87.[11]

It would be tempting for every player to deliberately choose a set of assumptions that would make everything come out as easily as he or she wanted. David Stockman, President Reagan's budget director, in fact became legendary for his manipulation of the "rosy scenario": a set of over-optimistic economic assumptions that made the president's promise of eliminating the deficit come true.[12] The budgetary game punishes players who toy too loosely with the projections. Choosing assumptions that are wildly out of line with all other players would destroy the player's credibility in all future budget battles. Most presidential budgets of the 1980s and early 1990s, in fact, were condemned as "dead on arrival" because Democratic members of Congress disagreed with their economic assumptions. The incentives are strong for each participant to choose assumptions on the happy side of the reasonable: numbers that are well within the bounds of the possible but that produce results favoring that participant's position. Since the battles of the 1990s, budget makers have squabbled less over the projections. That scarcely ended the political conflict, of course—they shifted their disputes to policy differences.

The Cycle of Economic Projections

The president's deficit forecast contained in each year's new budget, released in early February, is based on econometric forecasts produced in late December. It covers the period from October 1 of the next year to September 30 a year later—twenty-one months in the future. No one can know for sure, over that period of time, that the optimistic forecasts will not work out, so the incentives are strong to use them. Most of the time, the economy has refused to cooperate, and the deficits have surged ahead of the estimates.

More perversity creeps into the process when, as is almost always the case, the economic situation changes between the release of the president's budget in February and final congressional-presidential negotiations in the fall. Because such change is virtually inevitable, there is little incentive for anyone to negotiate seriously until the final numbers are known. Why should either members of Congress or the president play their best card if a minor, from a statistical point of view, burp in the economy can throw deficit estimates off by tens of billions of dollars?

It is little wonder, therefore, that neither Congress nor the president is anxious to complete its work on time. For purely technical reasons, careful negotiations completed early can be completely undermined by economic changes. In February 1990, President Bush produced a FY 1991 budget that would, he said, meet the Gramm-Rudman deficit target of $64 billion. By the time of the fall 1990 budget summit, the deficit had surged to $294 billion, a $230 billion increase caused mainly by the weakening economy in just ten months. The first year's cuts in Gramm-Rudman III brought the FY 1991 deficit estimate back down to about $250 billion, but the still-weakening economy drove it over $300 billion in the next six months. Over the long term, the message is the same. From FY 1980 to FY 1989, Congress's budget resolutions tended to underestimate the deficit by an average of $40.2 billion. Of this amount, $17 billion on the average came from mis-estimates of the economy's performance, and $11 billion on the average came from technical errors in the estimation process. As a result, Congress on the average underestimated the deficit by an average of more than $28 billion, purely because of problems in making good projections.[13] A decade later, the emergence of a recession in 2001 transformed a huge expected surplus into an unexpected and politically embarrassing deficit.

Budget makers thus can easily find themselves swamped by economic changes that overwhelm even well-intentioned efforts to cope with the deficit. Walter Wriston, former president of Citicorp, one of the nation's leading banks, notes, "A government budget deficit is the intersection of two wild guesses [on expenditures and revenues] a year from now."[14] It is little wonder that they pay so much attention to these guesses, to who makes them, and to trying to shape them in a way that minimizes the political costs as much as possible. It is also scarcely surprising that the intricacies of economic forecasting quickly overwhelm budgetary procedures.

Baselines

Complicating the problem of producing budget projections is the issue of the "baseline." As one of the most arcane parts of budgetary accounting, the baseline helps explain why spending more money might not be counted as a spending increase. Budget makers usually begin by estimating a "current services" baseline, that is, the cost of continuing each program next year at the this year's level of effort. To continue the program at the current level of effort, however, will often require an increase. Air-traffic controllers, for example, might receive a salary increase to cover the cost of inflation, or the cost of living might push up spending for social security. The baseline must also be increased to take account of more clients eligible for a program. If the medicare program receives more money simply because more individuals are eligible for the program this year, compared with last year, spending will go up but the program will not really "increase," at least in the sense of an expansion of new benefits.

These accounting peculiarities sometimes produce strange arguments. Agencies can receive significantly more money, but not really have an "increase," at least in the sense of an adjustment that allows for more services. Agencies spending more money this year than last can complain about cuts, if the increase is smaller than the inflation rate for their programs or the increase in the population they must serve. Likewise, budget bargainers can allow spending to go up, but at a lower rate than was projected, and claim they are reducing the deficit, because the increase is less than what it would have been at the higher rate. This can happen in part because revenues also tend to increase with inflation as well as with economic growth, and if the increase in spending can be held to less than the increase in revenues, the deficit will shrink. Budget "cuts" thus rarely mean reducing spending next year to less than was spent this year. Rather, they usually mean spending next year less than spending was originally *projected* to be.

Budget "cuts" also sometimes emerge even if Congress and the president actually end up spending more. Budget baselines are sometimes calculated on the basis of what spending has been approved, or even recommended, in the past. During the Reagan administration, for example, the president's budget offered big defense cuts, which in fact amounted to significant increases. The money requested was less than the administration's original and ambitious defense buildup planned but still more than inflation. To make matters worse, the key budget experts—the Office of Management and Budget and the Congressional Budget Office—often make different assumptions in calculating the baselines. Each agency prepares "baseline" budgets, based on the cost of continuing this year's programs next year at the same level of effort—and the baselines usually are different. Purely technical differences of opinion account for some of these differences. Occasional political judgments cloud the comparisons as well. It is hard enough to project future spending. It is even harder if the key participants cannot agree on where they are starting.

The fuzziness of the baselines further complicates budget making. Newspaper headlines that trumpet big cuts in federal spending can actually disguise spending increases. Increases in spending may not produce real growth in government programs, because inflation and more beneficiaries can quickly eat away at higher spending. To make matters worse, untangling all these issues requires considerable technical sophistication. The technical issues create a fog that makes it harder to judge what results budget negotiations are really producing and what is really happening to federal spending, year by year. Meanwhile, as with many other detailed technical debates, the battles over the baselines provide cover for clever participants to advantage some programs over others. Any time that differences in technical judgments produce political advantage, they never stay purely "technical" for long.

Process and Politics

Because negotiating the federal budget is so politically difficult and technically complex, everyone has a strong incentive to find some procedural solution to the problems. If only an automatic budget-cutting process could take control, the president and members of Congress could avoid direct political responsibility for the troublesome decisions that the budget presents. Perhaps increases in spending might be contained if the Constitution mandated that the budget be balanced or if the Constitution were amended to give the president greater authority to slice away pieces of the budget with which he disagreed. At an increasing pace, reformers are searching desperately for some alternative to the contentious battles that plague budgeting.

The promise of a procedural alternative to political struggle is alluring, but in the end it is impossible. There are, in fact, two lessons in the search for procedural reform. First, budgetary procedures simply cannot force budget makers to make decisions they wish to duck. Procedures can shape the way the debate is structured. They can define what is put on the table first, who is in charge of casting the alternatives, and what the political incentives are for cooperation. The history of budget reform, and particularly of Gramm-Rudman, is that there is no procedure that cannot be circumvented. Procedures are very important because of the way they shape the political contest, but they can neither determine the outcome of that contest nor even force the participants to play. Procedures simply cannot force elected officials to make decisions that they do not want to make.

Second, no process is politically neutral. Buried deep within every process is a subtle set of incentives, an intricate web of advantage and disadvantage. Gramm-Rudman III, for example, produced a massive shift of budgetary power from the Congress to the president simply by giving OMB the prime scorekeeping role. Every bit of the political process advantages some participants over others. Thus, it is predictable that the participants will promote the procedures that enhance their own power and seek to circumvent the procedures that give power to others. In budgeting, of course, this means that every debate over budgetary procedure is a veiled contest over the allocation of spending powers between the president and the Congress.

Thus, procedures alone cannot substitute for political judgments, nor can any procedure truly be politically neutral. Procedural reforms are never fully successful because they can never completely resolve the underlying political issues. They are almost always contentious because astute observers recognize the reallocation of political power typically buried within them. As attractive as it would be to solve the deficit mess through some new procedure, it is no more possible to do so than resolving the mess through some rational form of decision making. Politics is inescapably at the core of budgeting, and budgetary politics inevitably involves disputes over political power. Let us turn, then, to the critical disputes about power among political institutions, on which the deficit battles turn.

Notes

1. Allen Schick, *The Capacity to Budget* (Washington, D.C.: Urban Institute Press, 1990).
2. General Accounting Office, *Government Shutdown: Data on Effects of 1990 Columbus Day Weekend Funding Lapse* (Washington, D.C.: Government Printing Office, 1990), p. 11.
3. *Congressional Quarterly Almanac, 1985* (Washington, D.C.: CQ Press, 1986), p. 459.
4. This strategy represented a kind of "formula budgeting," in which mechanical rules were substituted for political judgments. For a discussion, see Eric A. Hanushek, "Formula Budgeting: The Economics and Analytics of Fiscal Policy under Rules," *Journal of Public Policy Analysis and Management* 6 (Fall 1986): 3.
5. For an examination of these issues, see Lawrence J. Haas, *Running on Empty: Bush, Congress, and the Politics of a Bankrupt Government* (Homewood, Ill.: Business One Irwin, 1990), esp. p. 8.
6. This summary is drawn from Congressional Budget Office, *The Economic and Budget Outlook: Fiscal Years 1992–1996* (Washington, D.C.: Government Printing Office, 1991), pp. 43–57.
7. Rudolph G. Penner, "Where Next for the Federal Budget?" *Policy Bites* (Urban Institute, December 1990), p. 1.
8. Ibid., p. 6.
9. Quoted in Haas, *Running on Empty*, p. 8.
10. Congressional Budget Office, *CBO's Economic Forecasting Record* (GPO, 2002).
11. Rudolph G. Penner and Alan J. Abramson, *Broken Purse Strings: Congressional Budgeting, 1974–88* (Washington, D.C.: Urban Institute Press, 1989), p. 99.
12. See David Stockman, *The Triumph of Politics* (New York: Harper and Row, 1986), p. 98.

13. Congressional Budget Office, *The Economic and Budget Outlook: Fiscal Years 1991–1995* (Washington, D.C.: Congressional Budget Office, 1990), p. 99. The other $12 billion error in estimating the final deficit came from policy changes made after the time of the projection.
14. Quoted in *Wall Street Journal*, August 21, 1986, p. 22.

CHAPTER 6

Congress, the Presidency, and Budgeting

Budgeting involves so many core issues in American society that it is inevitable that it becomes caught in a fierce struggle between the branches of government. If budgetary decisions are important, so too is the decision about *who* decides. Every important budgetary issue, in fact, focuses not only on the content of the policy but on the balance of power among American institutions, especially between the president and Congress. Our Founders, after all, designed conflict into our checks-and-balances system. As we shall see, they were only continuing a rich tradition of conflict between the executive and the legislative branches that stretches back eight hundred years or more.

The power to decide shapes the nature of the decision. The more power a president has over the budget, the more he can bend government programs to his point of view. The more power Congress and its members have over the budget, the more they can bring home the bacon to their districts. Furthermore, the ascendance of one branch in budgetary politics conveys great leverage over other important issues as well. A president who establishes his dominance by winning important budget battles will be hard to beat in non-financial issues, such as nominations for the Supreme Court justices or treaty negotiations. A Congress that can force presidential retreat in budgetary matters can search for other weaknesses in the presidential armor. This is especially true in a time of divided government, when the presidency and the Congress are controlled by different parties. Such divided government has characterized American government for most of the post–World War II period and only further increases the stakes about who makes budgetary decisions.

Some budget reformers have struggled to "fix" the process to minimize partisan conflict and, especially, disputes between the presidency and Congress. If history is any guide, that quest is impossible. One of the most fundamental problems of government is making it powerful enough to be effective yet responsive enough to the people to avoid tyranny. The search for governmental effectiveness has tended to enhance the role of executives, whether kings or presidents. Restraints on executive power by strengthening the voice of the citizenry has tended to enhance the role of the legislature, whether parliament or Congress.

The history of mankind's search for democracy hinges on these issues, and budgeting finds itself squarely in the middle. An executive who can tax can both increase his power and subdue his citizens. Taxing can limit the wealth of individuals, direct the labor of workers into certain directions, finance devices to control citizens (especially armed force), and more generally restrict individuals' freedom. The power to collect and spend taxes has always been at the core of executive power. Legislatures have arisen as people have tried to control that power. A fundamental dispute over the power to tax, in fact, lay at the heart of the uprising against King John of England in 1215, in which the nobles forced him to sign the Magna Carta. As one historian of the budgetary process, Jerry L. McCaffery, points out, of the sixty-one different articles in the Magna Carta, the most important was one that stipulated: "No scutage [a tax paid instead of having to serve in the military] or revenue shall be imposed in the kingdom unless by the Common Council of the Realm."[1] This agreement scarcely ended the disputes between the nobles and the king about who could impose taxes, but by the end of the thirteenth century, the principle of the supremacy of the Common Council (and later the parliament) was firmly established. As McCaffery points out, "the Crown had available only those sources of revenue previously authorized by Parliament."[2]

American revolutionaries themselves duplicated this principle 550 years later. Thomas Jefferson's Declaration of Independence renounced King George for, among other things, "imposing taxes on us without our Consent." When the war drove the British from the colonies, the new nation's leaders determined to prevent any repetition of such abuse of executive power. Under the Articles of Confederation, the Congress was dependent on the states for revenue. Taxation in the states, meanwhile, was largely in the hands of state legislatures. After the long and costly war, they were not eager to tax their citizens for the cost of a new government. The result was chaos, with an ineffective central government struggling to finance itself from stingy revenues raised by unwilling states. The Articles of Confederation produced enormous corruption and waste, and a clear lesson in how not to organize the nation's finances.[3]

In writing the new Constitution, Americans relearned some of the lessons of British history. Without a role for the executive in budgeting, effective execution of governmental programs was impossible. At the same time, too much power in the hands of the executive threatened a dangerous concentration of power. Putting the legislature in charge of approving expenditures maintained an effective check on executive power, but too strong a legislative role produced only chaos. The key, then, was to seek the right balance.

The Constitution split power, clearly but not cleanly, between the president and the Congress. The Congress was to have the power to raise money, while the president had the power to spend it. In Congress, either the House or the Senate could initiate new spending programs, but only the House could originate revenue bills. By keeping the power to tax in the part of the new national government with the strongest direct ties to the people, the Founding Fathers tried to contain the potential dangers that the power to tax posed. The president's spending power, furthermore, was limited to the programs enacted by Congress, as Congress enacted them.

At nearly every turn, the new nation fought against concentrating fiscal power. The new Treasury Department was the only new cabinet department for which a multimember board, instead of a single secretary, was seriously debated. Its first secretary, Alexander Hamilton, fought bitter battles to strengthen the national government, compared with the states, and to energize the executive branch, compared with the Congress. Secretary of State Thomas Jefferson and other Republicans contested his tactics at every turn. So bitter were the struggles, in fact, that his disputes finally cost him his life in a duel, with Aaron Burr, in 1804.

The Development of American Budgeting

Four threads thus combined to shape the new nation's finances:

1. The long British tradition, in which the legislature had ultimate power over revenue raising.
2. The unhappy American experience after the Revolution, in which it tried unsuccessfully to budget without an effective executive.
3. The Constitution, which sought to balance executive and legislative roles by splitting the power to tax from the power to spend and which limited the president's power to spend by the legislation enacted by Congress.
4. The new nation's rejection of the most ambitious elements of Hamilton's agenda, ensuring that the Congress was at the heart of budgetary politics.

These threads, however, left one important question dangling. How, in practice, was the balance between executive and legislative powers to be struck? In the two hundred years since, America has experimented with different answers, refined several principles, but in the end has never produced any solution that has long endured. Its history has evolved through three distinct phases.

The Era of Congressional Dominance: 1789–1921

For the first century of the American republic, Congress was the clear center of the budgetary process. Individual agencies submitted their spending requests directly to Congress, which decided agency by agency how much to approve. The president was hardly a disinterested bystander in the process. Several presidents, including John Quincy Adams, Martin Van Buren, John Tyler, James K. Polk, James Buchanan, Ulysses S. Grant, and Grover Cleveland, played important roles in amending agency requests before they went to Congress, and they sometimes dominated the process. Financing wars, especially the Civil War, gave the president a strong voice in shaping budgetary policy. Overall, however, budgetary decisions in the nineteenth century were the primary preserve of Congress.[4] There really was no "budget," in the sense of a coordinated plan detailing how much money was to be raised and how it was to be spent. Budgeting was largely an ad hoc affair, with the "budget" simply the accumulation of individual congressional decisions. As the country became larger and its programs more ambitious, however, congressional-centered budgeting began to lose effectiveness. To perform its work, Congress relied more on committees, and the committees in turn began relying more on subcommittees. Coordination between the tax-writing committees and the tax-spending committees began to break down. Each player in the congressional budget process began to act more independently. This "dispersal of responsibility," as administrative historian Leonard D. White put it, "made impossible any general view directed toward financial planning." To make matters worse, the decentralization of the system encouraged pork-barrel politics, in which individual members of Congress worried more about winning goodies for their districts than the overall shape of the budget. The result, as White explains, "was an extraordinary dispersion of responsibility for fiscal administration in the numerous offices concerned with public finance, and a corresponding confusion of responsibility for fiscal policy in an incompetent and badly organized legislative body."[5] The words are harsh, but the message was clear.

America's budget was becoming too complicated and its programs too important to operate without effective coordination. The lessons Hamilton had preached a century before began gradually to convince nearly everyone. Like other changes of the budgetary process, such as zero-based budgeting, reforms began bubbling up from state and local governments. After the turn of the century, the Progressive movement led many cities to establish budget offices in the executive branch. The states, starting with Wisconsin and California in 1911, followed the lead of the cities, and by 1926 every one of the forty-eight states had its own budget office.[6]

The Era of Presidential Dominance: 1921–1974

The federal government fell into line with the Budget and Accounting Act of 1921. The act did three things. First, it created the General Accounting Office, as a congressional agency, to review federal spending, including the expenditures made by executive-

branch agencies. Second, it created in the Department of the Treasury the Bureau of the Budget, to assist the president. Third and
most important, it empowered the president to submit an annual
budget to Congress. The act thus was a critical watershed in the
history of budgeting. For the first time, there was to be *a* federal
budget, a coordinated plan of spending and a statement of how revenues and spending would be related. Moreover, that plan would be
assembled by the president. The act thus dramatically changed the
balance of power between the president and the executive-branch
agencies, and between the president and Congress. Executive-branch
agencies would have to work with the Bureau of the Budget and the
president, instead of directly with Congress and its committees, to
secure their funds. Congress, furthermore, would now react to the
president's budget instead of framing its own policies in its own way.

This gave the president immensely greater leverage over the
entire executive branch. In a process that continues today, the Bureau
of the Budget (later moved to the president's own executive office
and renamed the Office of Management and Budget) began sending
instructions to executive-branch agencies about the overall framework of presidential policies. The budget bureau and the president
then reviewed the agencies' requests and considered how well they
fit the president's overall policy and more specific guidelines.
Requests that were out of line could be adjusted before being pack-
aged and sent, together with the president's budget message, to
Congress. The process thus began within a framework of the president's overall policies. Agencies had to fit within that policy or
demonstrate to the president why they should not—and the president had the last word. The budget package that the president sent
Congress set the agenda for congressional action, and the budget
message gave the president the opportunity to put all of the detailed
decisions over the budget into a broader framework. In the world of
public policy, the person who gets to set the agenda gains valuable
leverage over the rest of the process. The Budget Act of 1921 gave
that power to the president. It also gave him the muscle, through
creation of the Bureau of the Budget, to enforce it.

This important new leverage did not give the president complete
control over the process. Clever agency officials discovered, for
example, that they could increase their own budgets by appealing to

well-placed, friendly members of Congress who sat on the right committees. Such end runs allowed agencies to win more money without directly challenging the president. A conversation in a congressional hearing might work like this:

> *Friendly Member of Congress:* "You mean that the president's budget won't allow you to do your job as we've defined it in the law?"
>
> *Reluctant Agency Official:* "While we completely support the administration's position, it is true that the president's budget will not be able to meet all of the goals you'd like it to."
>
> *Friendly Member of Congress:* "Well, in that case, we might just have to increase your appropriation. Your programs [especially, he's thinking, the one in my district] are very important, and we want to make sure that they are run well."
>
> *Reluctant Agency Official:* "We'll do our best to meet the goals you have set for us [including protecting the programs in your district, since, the agency official thinks, that will help us next year if we need more assistance]."

Presidents and their budget officials, of course, are always on the lookout for such end runs. Those who try it can be punished in the next budget cycle, although Congress has more ways of creating such cozy relationships than top executive-branch officials have of stopping them. Many executive-branch officials, in fact, feel closer to the congressional committees that fund them than to the president, who is nominally head of the executive branch.

Overall, the Budget Act of 1921 marked a sweeping change in the relations between the legislative and executive branches. As Table 6–1 shows, it identified four phases to the budget cycle:

1. The *preparation* phase, in which the president and his budget office set preliminary targets for each agency, review subsequent agency requests, and then collect the final requests into a single presidential budget
2. The *appropriation* phase, in which Congress and its committees review the presidential requests and then enact the leislation to fund them, at the level Congress thinks appropriate

Deficit Politics

Table 6–1   The Budget Process

Preparation	Appropriation	Execution	Review
Summer: Preliminary budget "marks" sent to agencies by OMB			
Fall: Agencies submit budgets to OMB; OMB accepts, rejects, changes agency requests			
December/January: Final agency appeals to OMB director, and then to president	Late January: CBO estimates spending, taxes, deficit		
February: Submission of president's budget to Congress			
	April 15: Congress passes budget resolution, with targets for coming year		
August 20: OMB update on projected deficit	August 15: CBO update on projected deficit		
15 days after end of congressional session: OMB makes final deficit projection	10 days after end of congressional session: CBO makes final deficit projection		
	Congress enacts appropriations bills by the Oct. 1 start of fiscal year	Oct. 1–Sept. 30: Agencies manage programs as authorized by Congress	
			During fiscal year, and after: Agency performance reviewed by congressional committees and by GAO

3. The *execution* phase, in which the president oversees the executive branch's administration of the programs established and funded by Congress

4. The *review* phase, in which Congress—through its oversight committees and through the General Accounting Office, its audit arm—scrutinizes the way the executive branch executed the programs it funded; Congress reviews them both for financial integrity and for program effectiveness.

The budget process established in 1921 gave the president enormous new powers, by creating a unified presidential budget and strengthening the president's ability to oversee the agencies' execution of the budget. The president and his budget staff became the primary actors, and Congress reacted to them. The act thus marks one of the most important changes in the balance of power between the branches in the nation's history.

Ambitious presidential programs further strengthened the president's budgetary hand. President Franklin D. Roosevelt's aggressive plans for the New Deal required the development of ambitious programs and a strong executive branch to administer them. So, too, did his strategy to fight and win World War II. Later, President Lyndon B. Johnson's sweeping War on Poverty and his prosecution of the Vietnam War without a congressional declaration of war further enhanced the president's role as initiator and controller of national policy. The rising tide of presidential power peaked with President Richard Nixon, who advanced the use of the power of impoundment his predecessors had claimed: He refused to spend money that Congress had appropriated, especially for social programs favored by congressional Democrats. Members of Congress from both parties felt genuinely threatened by this assertion of presidential power. After all, if Congress passed a law and the president signed it but then refused to spend the money to administer it, what power would Congress have in the governmental process?

In the end, it was the very assertion of presidential power that led to attacks on it. Members of Congress were unhappy at President Johnson's prosecution of the Vietnam conflict without a declaration of war, and they were enraged at Nixon's impoundments. The balance of power between the presidency and the Congress reached

an unparalleled advantage for the president. Congress decided to try
to reestablish the balance.

The Era of Stalemate: 1974–Present

Members of Congress realized not only how strong the presidency
had become but also how weak and disorganized their own role in
the budget has grown. A report by the House Rules Committee in
1973 found that "the legislative budget machinery is in disrepair." As
a result, the report argued, "The excessive fragmentation of the
budget process in Congress makes it difficult for Congress to effectively assess program priorities or to establish overall budget policy."[7]

Congress as a whole—and Democratic members of Congress in
particular—took strong exception to President Nixon's assertion of
executive power. The impoundment dispute, of course, was part of
a much larger struggle that was part of Watergate. Congress's
response, the Congressional Budget Act of 1974, was likewise part
of a much larger effort to set a new balance between the branches.
The act made clear that Congress would not tolerate presidential
impoundment. If a president decides that he does not want to spend
money Congress has appropriated, he can ask for a "rescission," a
permanent decision not to spend the money which requires congressional approval. The act also gave him the right to defer spending money for a project until the end of a fiscal year, but even that
required the president to inform Congress. The act also changed the
start of the fiscal year from July 1 to October 1, to give Congress
more time to consider the budget.

More important, Congress created on Capitol Hill two important parallels to the presidential budgetary powers. While the 1921
budget act gave the president the power to propose a budget, the
1974 act gave Congress the power to assemble its own budget. Until
then, the budget passed by Congress was little more than the accumulation of decisions recommended by individual committees.
Those decisions, in turn, were shaped by the agenda framed in the
president's budget submission. There was no way for Congress, as
an institution, to consider the overall levels of spending and taxing,
to examine how different spending programs fit into the nation's
overall priorities, or to weigh the relative advantages of increasing

some programs more than others. Congress created for itself a new Committee on the Budget both in the House and in the Senate. The committee' job was to recommend a budget to the Congress as a whole, which Congress would then pass through a concurrent resolution. (Such a resolution requires approval by each house of Congress, but not the president's signature.) The budget committees would then set spending targets for each committee to meet the totals that Congress had agreed on. They would also keep score of the programs each committee approved to ensure that they remained within the targets. If committees exceeded their allocations, Congress could invoke a process called "reconciliation" to force the committees to reconcile their programs to the ceilings.

The 1974 act also attempted to help Congress match the president's budgetary staff help. The Bureau of the Budget, renamed and strengthened in 1970 as the Office of Management and Budget (OMB), gave the president a strong arm to use in enforcing his budget preferences. Congress tried to balance OMB's power by creating for itself the Congressional Budget Office (CBO) as the staff arm to the budget committees. CBO would study and report on the president's budget proposals. It would provide Congress with an independent judgment on the validity of the president's projections about the state of the economy and the costs of different programs. It would also keep score within Congress on how the results of individual committee decisions compared with the overall targets. Without a staff arm to match OMB, many members of Congress feared, the institution would always be at a disadvantage to the president.

The 1974 congressional budget act thus proved critical for evening the balance between the president and Congress on budgetary issues. Congress could counter the president's budget with its own plan. It could counter OMB's projections with those from CBO. It could prevent the president from refusing to spend money that Congress had appropriated, and it gained new powers to discipline its own committees. If not perfect, the balance was at least more even. As it became more even and neither the Congress nor the president were able consistently to dominate the process, however, passing any budget at all became harder. Since the passage of the budget act in 1974, Congress completed all of its work on the budget only twice, for the 1977 and 1989 budgets. In most other years, the process became entangled in conflict. Congress funded the government through a series of continuing resolutions, measures that temporarily extended the government's spending authority, until members and the president could agree on a new budget. Sometimes that took months. Occasionally it did not happen at all, and the government continued for the entire year on a continuing resolution instead of a regular budget.

Congress's reassertion of its spending power did not prevent presidential dominance, however. In 1981, for example, President Reagan and his budget director, David Stockman, skillfully used Congress's own procedures to push through the first year of the Reagan agenda. In particular, Stockman used Congress's own reconciliation procedures to force an up-or-down vote on the president's whole strategy.[8] The 1981 case proved important for two reasons. It showed the potential of a strong president to outflank a divided Congress. It also was one of the rare occasions since the passage of the 1974 act when any comprehensive plan was passed.

President Reagan's success in pushing through the 1981 budget, however, set the stage for subsequent deadlocks. The Democratic Congress, having been thoroughly beaten once, resolved not to allow it to happen again. The 1974 budget act gave the Congress more power to assert itself, but, by evening the balance, the budget reforms also made it more possible for each institution to block the other. With the decline of the norm of balance through the 1960s, running a deficit became more acceptable. With the decline of Keynesianism during the 1970s, it was unclear how large a budget deficit was too much. Now, with the rise of congressional power, the balance of power between the institutions became more even, just as budgetary decisions became ever more intractable. Conflicts became more fierce, the process broke down, and deadly duels erupted between the president and Congress.

Dealing with Deadlock

Presidential-congressional deadlocks thus became the standard operating procedure for the budgetary process. The budget game became one in which both the president and members of Congress maneuvered for position, struggled to avoid making decisions that would weaken their political support, and whenever possible sought to embarrass the opposition. It was a game of tactics without strategy, of a search for strong political positions without clear goals to guide them. At a time when no side—neither president nor Congress, neither Democrats nor Republicans—knew what it wanted, what each sought most was avoiding being backed by the other into a corner. The rise of the deficit during the Reagan years, coupled with the steady march of social security spending and ballooning expenditures for medicare and medicaid, made the game all the more dangerous. The possibilities for missteps multiplied as the room for maneuvering shrank.

Changes in Power Within the Branches

The maneuvers have subtly but importantly changed the distribution of power within the executive and legislative branches. Each change has altered the historic balance-of-power patterns.

THE EXECUTIVE BRANCH.   At least since the Nixon administration, presidents have struggled to gain leverage on federal programs by controlling spending. OMB has naturally been the centerpiece of this strategy. Nowhere else in the executive branch do all important financial questions come together, and nowhere else in the process does the president have such leverage. The result of the budget battles of the 1980s has been increasing centralization of power in the hands of OMB, and a growing political role for top OMB officials. David Stockman, President Reagan's OMB director, became legendary for his huge stacks of black notebooks, his calculator, and his role in negotiating for the administration. Richard Darman, President Bush's budget director, was the point man on each of the administration's budget battles.

Every important financial issue is increasingly funneled through OMB. Its creators intended the Bureau of the Budget, and then OMB, to play a staff role in supporting the presidential decisions. As budgeting became more important, OMB's director became a critical player in the direct chain of command. Over more than twenty years, the president's efforts to shape the budget and his struggles to resist congressional pressures have pushed OMB to the forefront. In the process, OMB has become both much more powerful and far more political, at least at the top. In fact, a very real gulf—both physical and psychological—has developed between the top OMB political officials, housed in the Eisenhower Executive Office Building on the White House grounds, and the OMB career staff, housed a block away and across a very busy Pennsylvania Avenue in the New Executive Office Building.

THE LEGISLATIVE BRANCH. Within Congress, the changes have been far more complicated. Recurring budget summits have shifted power from members of Congress and the committees to congressional leaders who do the negotiating. Congressional budget making thus is, in some ways, far more centralized than before the 1974 budget act, when the appropriations committees ruled Capitol Hill. It is also more centralized than in the years immediately after the passage of the 1974 act, when the budget committees exercised the most power. As congressional leaders learned the hard way in 1990, negotiating a budget deal they can sell to the rank-and-file is critical. Thus, overall, the increase in high-level budget summits has tended to centralize power in Congress the same way, and for the same reasons, as in the executive branch.

Compared with the 1960s and mid-1970s, important elements of Congress have lost power: the authorization committees (which create programs), the appropriations committees (which approve funding for the programs), and the budget committees (which are supposed to control the entire process). The authorization committees have moved toward approving programs for longer periods of time, which reduces their chance for oversight year by year. Meanwhile, more of the appropriations process is on automatic pilot. As we saw in Chapter 5, only about one third of the federal budget is subject to annual appropriations. Automatic appropriations for entitlements and payments for interest on the debt accounted for most of the rest. The increasing violation of Congress's budget schedule, finally, has weakened the budget committees. The process of determining overall budget targets and approving budget resolutions rarely happens on time. It is also increasingly meaningless when the real decisions are delayed to the very last moment before presidential-congressional negotiations hammer out a new budget.

The more Congress relies on continuing resolutions to keep government operating, and the more budget summits produce the real decisions, the more the budget committees fade from importance. Underlying this overall trend toward centralization, however, are some paradoxical shifts toward decentralization. Although the appropriation committees' power currently is far less than it was in the late 1960s, when the appropriations chairmen ruled supreme, the 1990 budget reform began increasing the committees' power once again. Gramm-Rudman III created tremendous pressure on discretionary spending as a whole, especially defense spending, yet it allowed a bit of maneuvering room for increases in discretionary domestic spending. The chairmen of the appropriations committees then had to balance which among the competing domestic programs would receive the little additional funding available. They also had to decide how the defense budget, in the aftermath of the collapse of Eastern Europe, the Iraqi war, and the ceilings imposed by Gramm-Rudman III, would be reshaped.[9] In fact, the more the budgetary process has become dominated by the megapolitics of budget summits and entitlements, the more pork-barrel politics have shrunk. What remains therefore is all the more valuable. The ability to deliver these projects has increased the power of the appropriations committees.

Overall, however, budget making in Congress has become less and less ordered. With authorizations made for longer periods, appropriations covering less of the budget, and budget resolutions rendered meaningless by last-minute summits, congressional budgeting is scarcely a textbook example of an ordered process. The result has been growing power for congressional leaders in hammering out the agreements. For Democratic leaders who have tended to control both houses of Congress, this means standing up to the White House, which has tended to be under Republican control. It also means negotiating carefully with Republican leaders, since the Democrats can rarely deliver the votes of all of their party members. For Republican leaders, this means working with the White House to establish a unified party position, embarrassing the Democrats when possible, yet treading carefully to avoid appearing obstructionist.

The congressional budget process has thus changed dramatically. Congress is regularly criticized for not producing its budgets on time, but the problem is not really a case of Congress's losing control. Rather, the breakdown of the congressional budget process is a very understandable response to the challenges of recurring large deficits, few easy answers, institutional battles with the White House over who controls the budgetary process, and fundamental struggles between the parties over who receives the credit—and more often the blame—for budgetary decisions. The simultaneous centralization and decentralization of the budgetary process is the natural result of the changing nature of the budget and budgetary politics.

Top-Down Versus Bottom-Up Budgeting

As the process has changed, the federal budget has been assembled more from the top down, instead of from the bottom up. In a bottom-up process, the budget is constructed by putting together the requests made by individual agencies. Top officials might shape broad policy decisions, encourage some agencies to seek larger requests and attempt to cut other agencies back, but the agency requests shape the budget. In a top-down process, the directives of the president and the budget office dominate. Several important trends have enhanced the importance of top-down budgeting:

1. The role of the deficit. In a world with expanding revenues and low deficits, responding to agencies' requests that float from the bottom up is easy. The high-stakes game of deficit politics, on the other hand, requires that the president and his budget staff regulate the expenditures of every federal program. As the deficit has grown, presidents have struggled ever harder to control it. The concept of the deficit has expanded from an accounting measure of the balance of expenditures and revenues to a far broader sign of presidential determination to control the size of government. The deficit has frequently been the focus of the struggle for power between Republican presidents and Democrat-dominated Congresses. For better or worse, the deficit has grown into a symbol larger than itself. Presidents must struggle to control it—or at least to appear to control it—and that increases the importance of top-down budgeting.

2. The rise of interest on the debt. Since interest payments doubled during the 1980s as a share of federal expenditures, a larger share of federal spending is determined simply by the pressures of financing the debt. That requires economic analysts to estimate how large the new deficit will be, how much the total debt will therefore be, how the debt will be financed, and how much the financing will cost. This is a complex set of calculations that can only be done centrally and decided from the top down.

3. *The rise of entitlements.* Likewise, a growing share of the federal budget is dictated by spending for entitlements, such as social security. Entitlement spending, of course, is determined by how many people are eligible for a program, what increases (such as cost-of-living adjustments) all recipients will receive, and what other changes in the program might be proposed or enacted. These calculations are extremely complicated and must be performed centrally.

4. *The debate over defense.* Like the deficit itself, defense spending has a strategic as well as a symbolic importance. Presidents sometimes seek to send messages to potential adversaries through the overall level of defense spending as well as through advocacy of new programs. The need for presidents to appear "tough" on defense, to "stand up" to potential adversaries can often have as much weight on the overall level of defense spending as the program-driven requirements of individual weapons systems. Broad strategic calculations and the symbolic message of "toughness" promotes top-down budgeting.

Spending issues have for centuries been the central focus of conflict between executives and legislators. The checks-and-balances system that has grown out of the English system of government, which we adapted in framing the American Constitution, envisions conflict as the critical element in preventing the abuse of power. Nevertheless, since the mid-1970s several features of deficit politics have intensified this conflict. Changes in the budgetary process have increased the balance between Congress and the president and, in doing so, have multiplied the opportunities for conflict. As the deficit acquired greater symbolic importance, the very structure of the budget made balance harder to achieve. Meanwhile, divided government—with Republicans in charge of the presidency and Democrats in control of both houses of Congress—became far more common than not. The result is a perverse cycle, in which the partisan conflicts increase the deficit, and higher deficits worsen the problems of divided-party government. As former presidential adviser Lloyd N. Cutler contended:

> High deficits occur when the President and Congress cannot form a consensus on a mix of taxes and competing expenditure programs that will create a reasonable balance between inflows and outflows. High deficits are the consequence of deadlock between the executive and legislative branches in the exercise of their shared power to legislate. In modern times high deficits have occurred only with divided government.[10]

We cannot conclude that ending divided-party government would solve the deficit problem, but it is certainly true that divided-party government worsens deficit politics.

Budgetary Policy and American Federalism

Often lost in debates over what the deficit does to relations between the president and Congress is the effect of the deficit on American federalism. When the federal government was financially more flush in the 1960s, it was a powerful engine driving innovation in the states and cities. Federal grants funded the construction of extensive mass-transit systems, the rebuilding of many central cities, the expansion of many social services, generous grants for education, and literally hundreds of other programs. Although these programs had many critics, including those who thought that the federal government had stuck its nose far too deeply into state and local affairs, most officials at all levels welcomed the federal government's largesse.

As the deficit began rising quickly in the late 1970s, however, federal grants suffered along with other domestic discretionary programs. Federal grants reached their high point in fiscal year 1978 and began shrinking (after accounting for inflation) thereafter. The one exception to this trend was the collection of federal grants for payments to individuals, especially medicaid, the federal government's program for providing medical care for the poor. Medicaid is administered by the states using money from federal grants as well as state sources. Federal grants, except for payments to individuals (most of which are for medicaid), decreased from 2.4 percent of the gross national product in fiscal 1978 to just 1.1 percent in fiscal 2001. Meanwhile, grants for payments to individuals grew significantly, from 1.1 percent of GNP in 1978 to 2.0 percent in 2001.[11] Discretionary grants to state and local governments suffered as much during the Reagan years as any other part of domestic policy.

Meanwhile, state and local governments found themselves subject to a dizzying variety of federal mandates. At a time when the federal government had little money to spend on domestic programs, it often found it easier to create policies and transfer their responsibilities to state and local governments. Some were not very costly, such as uniform speed limits and altering the drinking age to 21. In each case, the federal government could not order the states to make the change. The Constitution, after all, limits the federal government's role in state and local affairs. The federal government simply gave the states a choice: They could refuse to go along with the speed-limit and drinking-age policies, but if they did they would lose 10 percent of their federal highway grants. The states found that no choice at all and went along.

Some of the federal programs, however, were very expensive. The federal government, for example, dramatically increased clean-water regulations, including a requirement that local governments monitor their storm sewers to keep scores of chemicals out of the drinking water. Other federal mandates required school districts to eliminate asbestos from their buildings, increased state and local responsibility for protecting 152 new endangered species, and expanded the state role in inspecting the meat-processing industry. Meanwhile, the federal government preempted some state rules and imposed new direct regulations, such as labor standards, on state and local governments, even as the grants paying for many of these programs shrank. The General Accounting Office reported that "the overall pattern has been more federal involvement with less financial support."[12]

These mandates cut both ways. On one hand, federal mandates for medicaid are responsible for the fastest growing part of state government spending. In 1970, medicaid accounted for 3 percent of all state spending. By 1990, the amount had risen to 12 percent and was rising from 12 to 18 percent per year, far above the rate of inflation.

From 1988 through 1997, state spending for public welfare grew by two thirds. Most of this growth came from medicaid.[13]

On the other hand, some scholars have pointed out that the higher welfare benefits offered by some states create "welfare magnets" that draw poor people who might not otherwise live there. In 1985, for example, a three-person family living anywhere in Illinois received no more than $520 per month in welfare benefits. If they moved just across the border into Wisconsin, their benefits would increase by more than one fourth, to $662. The result of such a welfare policy is lower welfare benefits in some states, unsatisfactory choices of residence for many of the poor, and restricted employment chances for the poor who want to work. Paul E. Peterson and Mark C. Rom, who studied the problem, argue that the best solution is to create a uniform national standard for welfare benefits—that is, a mandated benefit floor. "A national welfare standard that gives poor people more residential choice can aid, however modestly, the increasingly concentrated child-centered poverty and at the same time ease competitive pressures on the states."[14]

The issues are difficult ones. As Peterson and Rom point out, federal mandates can sometimes make both the states and program recipients better off. The history of American federalism, furthermore, is that some states will always lag behind trends, whether in educational reform or in civil rights. Federal mandates provide a way to ensure uniform policies on questions of national interest. At the same time, however, the logic of mandates sometimes spills over into a vast array of issues whose cumulative impact, in state-local discretion and financial cost, is huge. Federal mandates are the engine driving up the most rapidly growing state expense, medicaid. So long as the federal deficit constrains national policy makers, mandates will remain attractive alternatives for policy makers who want to do something but who want to keep the costs out of the deficit debate.

Along the way, these strategies have significantly changed the relations among the nation's governments. The federal government relies ever more on state and local governments for administering its own programs, but at the same time there is persuasive evidence that federal mandates are undercutting the financial condition of the very governments it depends on. The federal budget cuts, the General

Accounting Office concluded, "helped to widen the fiscal gap between wealthier and poorer communities."[15] Meanwhile, tensions among the governments have increased along with the mandates. As state governments have become more important in managing domestic programs and in developing innovative solutions to public problems, the financial and regulatory burdens the federal government imposes threaten to undercut the states' important role. In a series of decisions separate from the deficit debate, the fallout from deficit politics has subtly worked important changes in federalism and in the vitality of state and local governments.

The Budget and Political Institutions

The budget and the budgetary process have changed significantly since the early 1970s. Budgetary procedures have broken down as partisan clashes between Democrats and Republicans have increased. Moreover, disputes over the allocation of budgetary authority between the Congress and the president have worsened fundamental debates hundreds of years old. The result of all this is a budgetary process in disarray—one in which conflict has increased and in which decision making has been increasingly centralized in both the legislative and executive branches.

These trends have also diminished public participation in the budgetary process. More budget decisions have been made by top officials in secret, last-minute negotiating sessions that give little opportunity for public input or reaction. This does not mean that public opinion is unimportant. The virulent public attack waged against the original budget summit proposal in 1990 to increase senior citizens' payments for medicare demonstrated that elected officials need to tread carefully. Such reactions, however, are rare because budgetary decision makers tend to stay far away from such contentious issues. Anticipated public reaction tends to define what will *not* be in a budget package. Broad public participation in actively shaping what *should be* in a deficit-reduction plan is rare.

Meanwhile, special interests have become more important in budget making. There is a long corridor outside the Senate Finance Committee meeting room, known popularly as "Gucci Gulch."

When tax provisions are up for debate, the hall is packed with highly paid lobbyists wearing Gucci shoes and carrying Gucci handbags, each one seeking to influence a narrow piece of the tax bill.[16] The more ad hoc the budgetary process becomes and the more it strays from predictable procedures set by a regular calendar, the more power such well-placed interests gain at the expense of other participants. Timing is everything in politics. In the heat of a last-minute budget battle, timing is critical. Good lobbyists who know whom to approach, how, and when are well worth the high fees they charge. Public participation thus does not disappear, but it becomes even more dominated than usual by those with an inside access to the process.

Deficit politics has sharpened the ageless conflicts between legislatures and executives, even as it has introduced important new problems. It has strengthened the hand of the president in searching for some order from the chaos. Partisan divisions between Democrats and Republicans, and thus often between Congress and the White House have, however, prevented the president from rising too far. Deadlocks have resulted, in part from the uneasy institutional balance of power between the president and Congress; in part from the partisan squabbles between Democrats and Republicans; and in part because the problem itself produces no easy answer. The struggle to deal with the problem has tended to centralize power in both the executive and legislative branches and to derail the regularly scheduled budgetary process. The rise of ad hoc budgetary politics has promoted the role of special interests and made most citizens even more distant—and increasingly cynical—observers of the most important issues of American politics.

Disputes between the president and the Congress are inevitable. Finding the proper balance between effective administration and popular control has always led to questions of how to set the balance between executive and legislative power. The issue dates from long before the American revolution, and there is no reason to expect that we will ever solve it. Conflict is the natural state of budgetary decisions, partly because the decisions are so important and partly because setting the balance over who makes those decisions is so difficult. At the same time, however, the disputes have become more rancorous, the results less happy over the last twenty years. There is one thread of the dispute that can never be resolved, but there is unquestionably an extra layer of conflict, produced by deficit politics. This new layer has affected the workings of American government to the core and has raised important questions about American democracy and governance.

Notes

1. Jerry L. McCaffery, "The Development of Public Budgeting in the United States," in *A Centennial History of the American Administrative State*, ed. Ralph Clark Chandler (New York: Free Press, 1987), p. 349.
2. Ibid., p. 350.
3. This story is well told in McCaffery, pp. 350–3.
4. See Louis Fisher, *Presidential Spending Power* (Princeton, N.J.: Princeton University Press, 1975); and McCaffery, pp. 359–60.
5. Leonard D. White, *Introduction to the Study of Public Administration* (New York: Macmillan, 1950), pp. 250–1.
6. Ibid., p. 253.
7. U.S. Congress, House of Representatives, Committee on Rules, *Budget and Impoundment Control Act of 1973: Report*, House Rpt. No. 93–658, 93rd Cong., 1st sess., 1973, pp. 21–2.
8. David Stockman, *The Triumph of Politics* (New York: Havper and Row, 1986).
9. Lawrence J. Haas, "Byrd's Big Stick," *National Journal* (February 9, 1991), p. 316.
10. Lloyd N. Cutler, "Now Is the Time for All Good Men . . . ," *William and Mary Law Review* 30 (1989): 390–1.
11. *Budget of the United States Government, Fiscal 2003: Historical Tables* (GPO, 2002), Table 6–1.
12. General Accounting Office, *Federal-State-Local Relations: Trends of the Past Decade and Emerging Issues* (Washington, D.C.: Government Printing Office, 1990), p. 26. See, more broadly, pp. 26–31.
13. David Merriman, "What Accounts for the Growth of State Government Budgets in the 1990s?" Report A-39 (Washington: Urban Institute, 2000) at http://newfederalism.urban.org/html/anf_a39.html (accessed February 12, 2002).
14. Paul E. Peterson and Mark C. Rom, *Welfare Magnets: A New Case for a National Standard* (Washington, D.C.: Brookings Institution, 1990), p. 138. The Wisconsin-Illinois comparison is drawn from Chapter 2.

15. GAO, p. 5.
16. A classic tale is about the Tax Reform Act of 1986. See Jeffrey H. Birnbaum and Alan S. Murray, *Showdown at Gucci Gulch: Lawmakers, Lobbyists, and the Unlikely Triumph of Tax Reform* (New York: Random House, 1987).

CHAPTER 7

Budgeting and Governance

Budgeting is quite naturally the lightning rod of American politics. The process of making taxing and spending decisions attracts and focuses every conflict in society. Every person with a cause, every group in need comes to budgeters. As budgeters make their decisions, moreover, conflict is inevitable because demands always exceed resources. Budgeting is, at its core, politics, and nothing represents the problems of politics better than budgeting.

Since the mid-1960s, however, the politics of budgeting has gotten far more difficult. Much of what government does, especially providing health care, income for the elderly, and national defense, has become far more expensive. Meanwhile, strong antitax feelings have made raising more money to pay for these services increasingly difficult. As elected officials have struggled to steer their way through often-impossible demands, they have had progressively less maneuvering room. The parts of the federal budget that have grown most quickly are those that are hardest to control. The parts of the budget that are easiest to control have been whittled down to the point where few obvious cuts remain. Meanwhile, subtle changes in tax policy have increasingly diminished the discretion that elected officials have. Changing the tax structure to bring in more revenue encounters bitter resistance at every turn.

So deep do the problems run, in fact, that it is tempting to see in the deficit a metaphor for the most fundamental problems of governance facing the nation. Congress and the president have, for years, been dancing an inelegant budgetary minuet, trampling upon each other's toes and many of our sensibilities. They ignore the deadlines of the budgetary process, often fail to produce a budget on time, protect their favorite projects while failing to deal with critical problems, and, to make matters worse, make halting progress at best in reducing the deficit. Are these issues signs of far deeper problems in our governmental system? Does deficit politics suggest that something is fundamentally wrong about governance in America? Put differently, can the budget problem be solved without restructuring the political system in some way?

Although the ongoing budgetary battles have a depressing familiarity about them, they are scarcely a symptom of fundamental breakdown of governance. As Daniel S. Ippolito argued, budgeting and governance are not identical. "The federal budget's elevation to a transcendent political issue has meant a lost sense of proportion about the problems it presents. The budget is important, but it is not commensurate with governance."[1] It is easy to confuse the two. When government workers go home and tourists must stare through locked museum doors, all because Congress and the president have been unable to agree on a budget and the government is shut down, it is tempting to regard the situation as a collapse of governance. On a symbolic level, of course, these events project powerful images. On a more fundamental level, however, they illustrate a set of false fetishes and enduring truths about budgeting and governance. Budgeting is part of governance, but governance is much more.

False Fetishes

Because so many issues swirl around budgeting, separating the critical budgetary issues from the fog that always surrounds budgetary battles is often difficult. The process of making spending and taxing decisions generates enormous conflict and proceeds at both highly symbolic and utterly practical levels. The symbolic politics of budgeting generates issues that seize the public agenda and dominate political debate, but in the end it detracts from the key issues that budgeters must solve.

The Search for Balance

No budgeting tale is more often repeated than the proverb, "A family must balance its budget. The federal government ought to do the same. If a family spends more than it takes in, it simply must cut its expenses. Here again, the federal government ought to do the same." Until well into the twentieth century, the federal government held to this norm. This is not to say that the federal government always ran a balanced budget. Deficits were frequent and, especially in wartime, frequently huge. Nevertheless, government decision makers and the people believed that the budget *should* be in balance. When it was not, because of war or a weak economy, they believed that the government should run a surplus to pay off the accumulated debt. Even if balancing the budget were not always possible, it always seemed desirable to try. Thus, when deficits became regular fixtures and reducing the national debt seemed impossible, it became easy to argue that persistent deficits were important signs of a failure of governance.

As we have seen, however, the federal budget is different from the family budget and, indeed, from state and local budgets. Because the federal government plays a critical role in stabilizing the economy, balance is neither always possible nor desirable. Furthermore, as leading economists have pointed out, we should not be fixated on balancing the federal budget. The primary role of the budget is to shape the economy, including the balance between government and the private sector; the allocation of goods and services among different groups of the population—rich and poor, old and young, urban and rural; and the allocation of out wealth between consumption in the present and investment for the future. The symbolic issues, especially the size of the deficit, are much easier to focus on, but the underlying questions are far more important—and more difficult to answer. The answers have become all the more difficult to find because as the norm of balance has disappeared, it has become ever harder to state clearly just how large a deficit is big enough—and how much is too big.

The lack of a budgetary balance thus is not important for its own sake. Rather, deficits are important because of what they mean for the way society uses its resources, both now and in the future. A large deficit can mean we spend too much money paying interest on the debt, that we are subsidizing the wrong groups in society, that we are living too high today at the expense of saving for tomorrow.

It is very easy, however, not to ask these questions but to use the deficit instead as a handy club to with which to beat opponents who

believe that the nation's wealth ought to be spent differently. The
deficit thus is a broad umbrella simultaneously covering many different issues. It rarely is easy to tell which issue really drives which
deficit arguments, but it is impossible to tell what deficit politics is
really about without understanding the underlying issues. The deficit
itself is a very real problem for much of American national politics.
Rarely, however, is the size of the deficit itself the central focus of
deficit politics.

Painless Cuts

When the consensus is that the deficit is too big but agreement on
reducing it seems so elusive, looking for painless cuts is alluring. The
news media regularly publicize tales of waste and suggest that there
might well be more where that came from. One ABC news investi-
gation, for example, uncovered a case where a Pennsylvania member
of Congress successfully won a $100 million appropriation for his
district to build an intelligence center for the war against drugs.
There already was a drug intelligence center in Texas, however. The
reporter used this as a premier example of waste in the government
that, when eliminated, would go a long way toward reducing the
deficit.

The reporter clearly believed that the United States did not need
another $100 million drug intelligence center. We might even agree
(although the member of Congress most certainly would not). We
cannot argue, however, that by systematically rooting out such programs we can make a serious dent in the deficit. Cutting even as large
a sum as $100 million out of a $1.25 trillion federal budget is the
equivalent of cutting $2.40 out of a family budget of $30,000. Such
cuts might add up if enough are found, but it is unlikely that a
family—or the federal government—could deal with a serious deficit
in its own budget by cutting out such spending. Agreeing on what is
"wasteful" is deceptively difficult. Tracking down such programs
requires resources, especially staff time, that are often very difficult
to obtain. If suspicion of criminal activity is involved, the investment
in prosecution is even greater.

The root cause of financial problems goes far deeper. As we have
seen, the strongest engines driving the growth in federal spending

are the entitlements, especially social security and, more recently, medical care (including medicare and medicaid). These are also the parts of the budget with the strongest political support. If budget makers are to reduce the deficit significantly by cutting programs, they must go where the money is, and this leads us back inexorably to entitlement and defense programs. The easiest and most attractive answers, such as the horror stories sprinkled through the news media, perversely produce little realistic savings. The few places large enough to absorb substantial cuts lie on the budgetary turf that is most strongly defended.

On a rhetorical level, elected officials often find it attractive to deal with the deficit as a problem of cutting waste, fraud, and abuse. They can argue they can make real progress without hurting anyone except those who deserve to be hurt. The real truth, however, is that the causes of the deficit run far deeper. There are only three ways of reducing the deficit: raising taxes, cutting spending, and encouraging economic growth. The deficit itself tends to restrain economic growth, we resist tax increases, and making significant spending cuts runs afoul of strong interests protecting the defense and entitlement budgets. This does not mean that real deficit cutting is impossible. It does mean that genuine progress in reducing the deficit can never be easy or painless. In the face of such difficult decisions, it is little wonder that the political process is so contentious or that political institutions show signs of strain.

"No New Taxes"

The decade of the tax revolt, starting in the late 1970s in California and bubbling upward to George Bush's bold "no new taxes" pledge, clearly established that Americans are fed up with taxes. Nevertheless, as we have seen, the very complexity of the deficit problem suggests that taxes need to play some role if the deficit is to be reduced. Buried in the revolt over taxes, however, are subtle changes that make building support for deficit reduction through tax increases hard. One is that a larger percentage of the federal tax burden has shifted to individuals from corporations. For individuals, the tax burden has shifted more to the payroll tax, which hits lower-income wage earners the hardest. Similar changes are occurring at the state and local level as well. Voters are angry and have signaled clearly that they do not intend to take it any more.

At the same time, there has been an increasing disconnection between the taxes that workers pay and the benefits they receive (or at least that they *perceive* that they receive). The increase in payroll taxes on today's workers, for example, has gone largely to pay for an increase in income and medical benefits for today's retirees. Federal individual income taxes about equal the expenditures for national defense and interest on the debt. The sense of a growing tax burden, felt especially by the middle class, is even more painful because the middle class does not associate it with more and better government programs.

Little wonder, then, that the "no new taxes" theme resonated so clearly among Americans. The taxpayers who are bearing most of the burden do not see much direct benefit from the taxes they pay. Much of the money goes for a transfer between generations, from younger workers to retirees; for broad public goods such as national defense, from which everyone benefits but where the direct benefit for most taxpayers (except military contractors and members of the armed services) is relatively invisible; and for the cost of keeping government in business, especially interest on the national debt, which seems on the surface to produce no real benefit at all. It is hard for budget makers to campaign for higher taxes if those who will pay most of the taxes do not see an increase in services the government provides them. This trend only more firmly cements in place the basic problems—and makes solving them ever more difficult.

Protected Entitlements

For most Americans, entitlement programs—principally social security, medicare, and military retirement programs—represent a sacred social contract with which elected officials ought not tamper. Not all entitlements go to the elderly, but payments to retired persons dominate entitlements. This dominance will increase, furthermore, as the population ages and retirees live longer. The social contracts at the bottom of entitlements, however, are more a political than a moral construction. Their continued budgetary success is a monument to a complex set of interrelated themes: the great service that today's generation of retirees gave the nation in several wars; ambitious presidents and Congresses seeking to improve the living conditions of Americans, especially the elderly; a generation of rapid economic growth that has made relatively rapid expansion of these programs possible and relatively painless; the much higher voter turnout among retirees than of any other group of the population; the eagerness of retirees to punish elected officials who dare even consider cutting these programs. Having worked hard to build the American dream, many retirees believe that the nation now ought to make good on its promise.

One easy way to reduce the deficit would be to honor the letter of this social contract, to repay today's retirees what they contributed during their working lives. Virtually everyone on social security and medicare so far has gotten back more than they paid in, and the same is true for recipients of other retirement programs. Regularly increasing program benefits, whether through automatic increases indexed to the cost of living or expanding the program's base, has been an irresistible way of building political support among a group of the population that votes loyally in large numbers. In the process, they have rolled ever-greater promises into the social contract. The cost of the contract has grown enormously, but at the same time the promises have become sacred and politically untouchable.

This does not mean that the claims of retirees are not valid. One can scarcely question the use of our great national wealth to lift senior citizens up out of poverty. The nation owes a great deal to the generation of Americans retiring in the 1970s, 1980s, and 1990s. This was the generation that fought World War II and the Korean War. It was the generation that built the United States into a major world economic and political power. It was the generation that constructed the remarkable engine of economic growth that has so substantially improved the living conditions of every American. One can question, however, whether money spent on entitlement programs for senior citizens ought automatically to enjoy a privileged place in the budget. Should the needs of senior citizens have a higher claim on the nation's wealth than the need, for example, to provide food and education for today's children, to build the nation's basic infrastructure for the future, or to invest for tomorrow's economic growth?

Through the budgetary process, the answers emerge in political terms, based on the political strength that senior citizens have amassed. In fact, a hierarchy of budgetary claims has emerged as the structure of the budget has changed. Interest on the national debt must be paid first. Entitlement spending, especially for social security and medicare, comes next and is virtually untouchable. There is near-universal agreement on the need for a strong national defense, but countless quarrels over just what level of defense spending is enough. Other programs, including discretionary domestic programs, follow behind in this hierarchy.

Both budget analysts and those with other political interests might argue that this is not the best way for the nation to allocate its wealth. The reality, however, is that the hierarchy of political claims on the budget is strong. The changing shape of the budget, coupled with changes in the budget-making process itself, such as the 1990 budget reforms, makes it very difficult even to ask the question. Thus, the basic questions of deficit politics cannot be answered without understanding the important financial and political role that entitlement programs play. Reducing the deficit and, especially, investing for the nation's future economic growth, leads inevitably to reconsidering whether entitlements deserve their privileged place in the budgetary hierarchy. This shocking question immediately creates an enormous political battle. Without thinking through these issues, however, the nation is committed to an intergenerational chain letter that cannot be perpetually continued.

Eternal Crisis

The eternal crisis of the budgetary process is the best evidence of fundamental problems of governance. For decades, ambitious and much-praised reforms have led to new budgetary crises. Budgets rarely have been adopted according to schedule, and the president's budget has regularly been declared "dead on arrival," except when critics call it "dead before arrival." Battles seem eternal, truces are elusive, and lasting answers to the critical issues never develop. If budgeting is the core of politics, and if Congress and the president cannot seem to budget, perhaps the problems do indeed represent a basic problem of governance. However, as easy as it might be to see in recurring budgetary crises a discouraging breakdown in the American governmental system, the reality is nothing of the sort. The real issues are much larger—and much smaller—than simply a breakdown of the process.

Enduring Truths

The budget, of course, is critically important in itself. Anything so large, amounting to one fourth of the nation's total production of goods and services, demands attention for its own sake. More important than the budget, though, is what the budget is used for: to redirect the nation's wealth, among groups of the population today, and from uses today toward investments for the future. In addition to these grand-scale questions, the budget also embodies a host of smaller ones, including how the process itself works. Our exploration of these issues leads us to important, enduring truths about budgeting.

The Budget Is Inevitably Political

As long as budgeting has been important it has seemed sloppy. Side deals are cut, deadlines are missed, critical programs are not funded, and wasteful pork-barrel projects sometimes receive money instead. It is little wonder, then, that reformers have long looked for some philosopher's stone that would show the right way to deal with these tough questions—for some grail whose elixir would clear the mind and point decision makers on the best path. Reformers have, in short, always looked for some way of making decisions that would replace politics with rationality, some way of structuring the process that would impose order on the unruly pulling and hauling of budgeting.

This crusade is doomed to failure. Some approaches to more rational decision making can indeed improve the way the budgetary process works, by structuring the way decisions are made and by improving the information that budget makers use. Changes in the budgetary process can improve the chances for agreement.

Rationality, however, can never replace politics. Budgeting is about making choices, and making choices is impossible without discriminating among competing values. Choosing among competing values, of course, is what politics is all about.

Every "rational" approach is, in fact, a way of emphasizing some values over others, of empowering some players more than others, of favoring some outcomes more than others. There is thus a subtle perversity in the search for rationality. It is an impossible dream. The process of searching for it, furthermore, always favors some results over others. There is no way to avoid politics in budgeting, because budgeting is at its very core political. Realizing that, budget makers need to be suspicious of any crusader who promises a way to avoid making the difficult decisions, for any magic solution can never be anything more than a masquerade for fundamental value—that is, political—choices.

The Structure of the Budget Affects the Budgetary Process

Since World War II, the pieces that make up the federal budget have gradually, sometimes imperceptibly, changed. We have laid out the broad sweep of these changes: roller-coaster trends for defense spending; rising expenditures for interest on the debt; even more rapidly growing spending for entitlement programs, especially for the elderly; and a shrinking share for everything else. These changes are a result of the changing constituencies for federal programs, as the nation has grown both older and more affluent. Government has, since World War II, moved rapidly past the traditional role played by government to new social responsibilities, especially in income support and health care.

As new constituencies have won a growing piece of the federal pie, however, the process itself has become afflicted with budgetary arteriosclerosis, a hardening of the categories. The disease makes budget decisions more difficult because each succeeding group of budgeters has less discretion than the one before. More of the budget is on automatic pilot, determined by the need to finance the debt, entitlements, and existing contractual obligations. The share of the budget open to discretionary choices by budget makers is shrinking steadily.

Changes in the tax system, meanwhile, have enlarged the burden on individuals and produced the call for "no new taxes." Any increase in revenue must therefore be disguised as something that does not look like taxes. In 1989, for example, President Bush's budget director, Richard Darman, invited reporters to apply the "duck test" to the newly elected president's first budget. If it looks like a duck, walks like a duck, and quacks like a duck, he said, then it must be a duck. Likewise for taxes. By the time the Bush administration's budget battles ended, observers could not resist quacking. Like his predecessors before, President Bush found that he had to accept tax increases. He had few other choices.

The structure of the budget shapes budgetary politics in several important ways. It defines who the important players are. It has established the hierarchy of claims on the budget. It has increasingly separated the raising of money from its spending. It has shrunk the flexibility of budget makers to shape solutions to new problems and, if they do attempt to create new programs, it imposes a heavy political cost for doing so.

In short, the changing structure of the budget has tended to load the process in favor of the winners of past battles. Even the "pay-as-you-go" procedures adopted in the 1990 budget act, which created at least the possibility of new and expanded programs, actually creates a double barrier: winning support for the programs, and then finding the money to pay for it. The "firewall" between social security and the rest of the budget, as well as the breakdown of discretionary spending into defense, international, and domestic categories, has also tended to keep the levels of spending relatively fixed. At the same time, budgetary categories have made it ever harder for new players even to get into the game. Those with a place at the table have strong incentives, and great ability, to keep it. Those who do not have a very tough job in winning a seat.

The Budgetary Process Affects the Distribution of Power

The logical corollary of this point is that the budgetary process and structure shape who has power in the process. In part, this means that those who win shape future debates. Social security, for example, was not always the "third rail" of American politics—"touch it and you die." Proposing increases in medicare fees was not always a prescription for creating problems. As the populations benefiting most from the changes in federal spending have grown, and as their budgetary success has increased, so too has their political leverage over the process.

Changes in the process have also affected the distribution of power among American political institutions. The national government's growing intergovernmental role has led to an expansion of federal grant programs for medicaid and other payments for individuals. This financial leverage over state and local governments has led to more mandates over how state and local governments must spend their money and, in the process, a centralization of substantial power in the hands of the national government. The national government, in fact, has acquired influence not only about what state and local governments must do but also about how they must do it. It has also gained the power to transfer national costs to state and local budgets. In this is yet another paradox. The cutbacks in discretionary domestic spending, especially at the beginning of the Reagan administration, led many state and local governments to much more creative government. Their policy initiatives and energetic management have often become models that the national government has itself come to follow. While this energetic new role was evolving, however, national control over state and local budgets has increased. Nationally orchestrated changes in the medicaid program have created one of the most rapidly growing parts of state government spending, for example.

In Washington, changes in the budgetary process have also dramatically altered the relationships among the branches of government, notably Congress and the president. Constant budgetary battles unquestionably have soured the ties between the branches and created ill will that spilled over into other issues. Reforms in the budgetary process, including the Congressional Budget Act of 1974 and the various versions of Gramm-Rudman, first increased Congress's role in the process. As Congress gained more power, however, conflict between the president and Congress has increased. Growing partisan battles between the branches have led to subtle reforms, such as increasing OMB's role as budgetary scorekeeper, that have gradually shifted power back up Pennsylvania Avenue to the

White House. The president's power to propose the budget, shape the issues, launch initiatives, choose economic projections, and especially to blame Congress for what goes wrong, has steadily enhanced the executive branch's power. Most members of Congress have found themselves back in the role of reacting to the president's initiatives.

Process changes have also shifted the distribution of power within the branches. In both branches, the primacy of budgetary politics has focused enormous energy at the top on the key issues, such as the size of the deficit and the shape of major spending programs. Within the executive branch, this trend has enhanced the growing primacy of the Office of Management and Budget. OMB has become the nerve center for the executive branch's budget strategies and tactics. It has grown far past the limited staff arm envisioned when it was created in 1921 to the central executive-branch clearing house for all financial matters. Leverage over money, of course, has given OMB enormous power over the details of policy. In regulatory as well as spending issues, OMB's power has grown enormously as budget crises have recurred.

At the same time, the operating discretion left to executive-branch agencies has paradoxically increased. The president and OMB can only fight a few key battles, and as the battles have grown more important they have occupied more time. As government programs, from researching a cure for AIDS to governing the air-traffic control system, have become more complex and the ability of top-level officials to oversee these activities has shrunk, the agencies and bureaus have gained more discretion. Thus, changes in the budgetary process have promoted simultaneous centralization and decentralization in the executive branch.

The same has occurred within Congress. Frequent budget summits have increased the power of top congressional leaders, as they attempt to forge an agreement for the members of their parties. They cut the pivotal deals, agree to the significant policies, and exact the important concessions. Then they face the job of selling the plan, even as party unity within Congress has declined. The job of filling in the many details of the overall plans, as well as dealing with most other matters Congress must decide, is left in the hands of Congress's many committees and subcommittees. The appropriations committees in both houses have, in particular, regained substantial power that they had lost in earlier budget reforms as they have sought to make the difficult trades in discretionary programs required by the category-by-category caps introduced by the 1990 budget act.

Thus, changes in the budgetary process have changed political power in three important ways: (1) These changes have enhanced the role of important political constituencies who are already part of the game while making it even harder for marginal players to gain a seat. (2) They have strengthened the hand of the White House while making it more difficult for Congress as an institution to maneuver. (3) Finally, they have simultaneously centralized power in both branches over the critical policy decisions and decentralized power over many details. Future budget reforms undoubtedly will change these relationships yet again and underline the basic lesson: The budgetary process is about more than just how the budget is formed. It is also critically about *who* gets to decide budgetary issues.

Economic Projections Have Inordinate Power

To many budgeters, the most frustrating change in budget making since World War II has been the growing importance of economic projections. Budget makers increasingly have little incentive to play their hand in negotiations until the shape of the economy is clear. Even minute changes in economic performance can, virtually overnight, upset budgetary compromises. The American economy itself has become more unstable and more interconnected with the global economy. Any change anywhere can spill over into the American economy more easily than ever before. Moreover, as more of the budget has become indexed to economic conditions, these economic conditions affect more of the budget directly. Hard-fought deals can be undercut within weeks by an economic hiccup.

These projections are also politically important because more of the key players have their own computers, models, and data. They can produce their own projections, based on their own assumptions, and vie with other participants for more favorable treatment. Unscrupulous players in the budgetary game can decide which outcomes they want and choose their economic assumptions accordingly. The proliferation of economic models and modelers helps keep everyone more honest, because such attempts to rig the game quickly become obvious. Nevertheless, with more of the budget determined by economic projections and more participants on the budgetary process equipped to duel with competing projections, the technical side of budgetary politics has taken on far greater importance than it had decades ago.

Budgeting: Politics at the Highest Level

Budgeting is the nerve center of the political universe—and it can often seem that this center is in chaos. Such chaos results from the most basic truth of budgeting. Budgetary politics lies at the intersection of the critical issues in American government, issues that usually tug in opposite directions. We want strong control from the top (which argues for a powerful executive role), yet we want to ensure that the process is responsive (which argues for a strong legislative role). We demand extensive government services but usually resent, of course, having to pay for them. If we feel entitled to these services, we expect that they will be provided regardless of other circumstances, yet we demand that tax dollars be allocated to society's unmet needs.

We simultaneously want centralization and decentralization, consistent rational answers coupled with great political responsiveness, low taxes and high spending, a strong president and an effective Congress, a smooth process that substitutes predictable steps for political conflict, a balanced system of federalism along with state and local responsiveness to nationally defined goals, a rational system with a clean process, an energetic national economy that saves for the future. In short, we want everything, yield on nothing, and are prepared to complain bitterly when our preferences clash with anyone else's. It is little wonder that the system looks chaotic, for conflicts are everywhere. It is also little wonder that the closer we look at budgetary politics, the more it might seem a symbol for fundamental problems of governance.

No Easy Fixes

Understanding budgeting means understanding that decisions about taxes and spending focus in one place the most important and most divisive issues in the political system. Budgeting sharpens debates over the balance of powers among parts of the system and acts as a magnet for society's conflicts. If budgeting is contentious, the problem is not so much budgeting but the questions it must answer. Budgeting is a mirror held up to the political system. By looking into that mirror we learn as much about the political system as we do about budgeting itself.

In framing our system of government, the Founding Fathers taught an interesting lesson. When they faced unresolvable problems, they did not try to eliminate the conflict. Instead, they sought to structure the conflict in such ways that strong feelings could be heard and competing opinions could be balanced. The genius of the founders lay not in *solving* the new nation's problems but in *structuring the conflicts* so they could be solved. Some changes in the budgetary process might well reduce conflict. Using a consensus economic forecast instead of having each participant conduct computer-based forecasting duels might establish a common ground on which budget makers could work. Moving even more toward a more comprehensive budget, and away from the trend to segregate different parts of the budget in self-contained packages, would ensure that budget makers face the full consequences of their decisions. Moving away from measuring budgetary decisions in terms of deficits—the combined effects of this year's spending and revenues— toward longer-term measures of what the nation spends might improve the process. Budgeters might then be less tempted to shift programs back and forth among different budget years simply to affect this year's deficit estimates and would be forced more to confront the real costs of what they are spending.

In technical terms, controlling government spending means worrying much more about *budget authority*, the amount of budget Congress appropriates (regardless of when the money is spent), than about *outlays* (the amount of money spent in any given year). Government spending is measured in terms of outlays, which might not necessarily measure well the obligations to which the government is committing the nation.

These procedural reforms, of course, are very modest. The more basic struggles cannot be eliminated because they mirror basic conflicts in American society. This is why we cannot simply "fix" the budgetary process, for so long as these underlying conflicts exist budgeting itself is inevitably quarrelsome. Making budgeting smooth and easy would require reducing political conflict in the American system as a whole. There is nothing fundamentally wrong with the budgetary process that easier decisions would not solve. So long as there is disagreement in the nation, it will find its way into the budgetary process.

Understanding the Varieties of Budgeting

A constant theme in this journey through budgeting is that the variations in budgeting are as interesting as the common threads. We can examine the types of budgeting in two ways: cutting budgeting *horizontally*, by understanding how budgeting varies among different kinds of programs; and cutting budgeting *vertically*, by understanding how budgeting varies at different levels of government.

HORIZONTAL CUTS. Different kinds of programs have different kinds of budgetary politics. Budgeters responsible for determining the social security budget, for example, must estimate how many new recipients will be coming into the program in any given year, how many existing recipients will die, and what the benefit for each recipient will be given past work histories and current benefit levels. The law sets the expenditure for each recipient. Calculating the budget for such entitlement programs is then a technically complex but conceptually straightforward matter of running the Social Security Administration's computers.

On the other hand, determining how much aid the federal government ought to give to college students or how much money the federal government ought to spend in AIDS research is a matter of delicate political maneuvering. Since these are discretionary programs, the president and members of Congress must weigh competing priorities, past political commitments, and emerging needs. Then they must decide how large a piece of the pie, sometimes shrinking in size, to devote to such programs. Budgeting for discretionary programs thus is a matter of bargaining. In between is the defense budget. Some defense issues carry important symbolic value, such as how large a fighting force we wish to project or which new weapons system we wish to begin. Some issues are predetermined, such as previous contractual commitments for buying weapons. Other issues are mundane, including calculating such apparently trivial but actually very expensive matters as the food and utility costs for American bases around the world.

Budgeting thus varies tremendously from program to program. There are different kinds of politics for entitlement, defense, and discretionary programs. Any approach to understanding budgeting must account for these differences.

VERTICAL CUTS.   Budgeting is also different depending on the level of the system. At the very top, the president, his principal advisers, and congressional leaders haggle furiously over the overall shape of the budget: the total level of spending and taxing; major policy initiatives; and, of course, the size of the deficit. Their perspective on budgetary politics is largely conceptual and symbolic. Most of the information contained in the 2.5-inch thick federal budget is irrelevant to the few critical questions that top-level officials must settle. From their point of view, budgeting is a top-down affair. They expect to make the key decisions and then to allow the implications to filter down through the rest of government.

Conversely, the size of the deficit and other grand-scale issues is mostly immaterial to operating officials throughout government— the part of government represented in most of the budget's thickness—except as the deficit affects the amount of money they have to spend. These officials are concerned with making their programs work, whether processing social security checks, launching space missions, cleaning up the environment, catching criminals, or conducting medical research. It is the task that determines their focus, and this task-oriented perspective creates a bottom-up approach to budgeting. They analyze how much money is required for them to complete their mission, as defined in laws passed by Congress and signed by the president. They may or may not get the money they ask for, but from this perspective budgeting is driven by mission requirements.

Budgeting thus is different at different levels of the political system. There is a different kind of politics, a different set of goals, and widely varying perspectives on the basic problems. Just as any approach to budgeting must account for differences among different kinds of programs, it must also account for variations among different levels of the system. Here again, budgeting provides a useful prism for understanding important issues in how government works.

Governance and Leadership

One of the deepest conflicts in budgeting is the struggle for power and advantage prompted by divided-party government. Americans have since the late 1960s often elected members of Congress and presidents of different parties (which has usually meant Democratic congresses and Republican presidents). The parties have frequently sought to define their differences in budgetary terms: defense versus domestic spending, protecting versus cutting social security, tax increases versus no new taxes. As the structure of the budget has become less flexible, budgetary politics has tended to exacerbate the conflicts flowing from divided-party government, and the struggles between the parties have in turn worsened budgetary battles.

The answer to these battles in the end is not less but more partisanship.[2] The primary function of parties and political leadership in society is to define our problems, shape our choices, and build support for answers. We cannot expect to eliminate controversy. Indeed, the closer we come to asking fundamental questions, the more controversy is likely to increase. If the message of more than two centuries of American democracy is any guide, that is both inevitable and necessary.

And here we get to the heart of the problem. We must ask what deficit battles tell us about our system and our values. We must see them as challenges to our political leaders. Governance is the process of resolving these conflicts. This comes from political leadership, and leadership requires the articulation of a broad vision for where society will go. When leadership is lacking, when the vision is narrow, the conflicts can scarcely be resolved. We must also see the deficit battles as challenges to our own sense of fairness, our own sense of what the pursuit of the public interest—instead simply of our individual interest—requires.

That, indeed, is the lesson of this book. It is tempting to seek answers to the problems of the budget in procedural fixes and other Band-Aid efforts. But at the core of the budget's problems is politics, and politics always means conflict. The structure and processes of the budget are most certainly not neutral, but neither can the broad political issues be resolved simply through structural or procedural change. Political conflicts can be resolved only by political leadership. It is tempting to encourage elected officials to appeal only to our narrow individual interests. The highest obligation of citizenship, however, is to challenge leaders to appeal to a much larger obligation, to serve the broad public interest. It is here that deficit politics, budgeting, and governance all combine. Budgeting tells us much about our system of government, our system of government tells us much about budgeting, and both combined tell us much about ourselves.

Notes

1. Daniel S. Ippolito, *Uncertain Legacies: Federal Budget Policy from Roosevelt Through Reagan* (Charlottesville: University Press of Virginia, 1990), p. 231.
2. Ibid.

Index

177